KEEPER OF THE FEMALE MEDICINE BUNDLE

Biography of Wihopa

Denver - Wicòni Wastè Publishing

Reprinted by Color House Graphics, Inc. for
Allen Ross
P.O. Box 480005
Denver, Colorado 80248
Copyright © 1998
by Allen Ross

First Printing - February 1998
Second Printing - April 1998
Third Printing - June 1999
Fourth Printing - January 2000
Fifth Printing - November 2000
Sixth Printing - June 2002
Seventh Printing - August 2003
Eighth Printing - December 2005
Ninth Printing - May 2007
Tenth Printing - June 2009
Eleventh Printing - July 2010
Twelfth Printing - June 2011
Thirteenth Printing - July 2011
Fourteenth Printing - August 2012
Fifteenth Printing - October 2013

LIBRARY OF CONGRESS CATALOGING IN PUBLICATION DATA.

Ross, Allen
Keeper of the Female Medicine Bundle
Bibliography: p. 244
CIP#98-90048

ISBN 0-9621977-7-7

ACKNOWLEDGEMENTS

All American Indian Women

All Sun Dancers

My Parents: Harvey & Agnes Ross for their support and
                   direction.

My Wife: Dorothy Brave Eagle for her patience, under-
                   standing and love.

Susan Koyama: For her interview with Wihopa - Agnes Ross.

Cover Artist: Lyn Aus Roy

My Astrologer: Mary Jayn - for her wisdom and knowledge.

My Typist: Debbie Stuck - for her editing and guidance.

Michael Kastner: Dorothy's Hunka brother for his support.

All my children and grandchildren.

My brothers for their input on Section 2.

My brother Jim Bill for his research on the family tree.

My Hunka Children: Amber No Horse
                           Ralphie Hernandez
                           Kristi Blue Bird
                           Chaske Luger
                           Elgin Head
                           Stanley Natchez
                           Florentine Blue Thunder
                           Joe Marino
                           Sandra Rolshoven

Table of Contents

The Last Keepers of the Female Medicine Bundle

Hupahu sna sna win
(Rattling Wings Woman)
1827 - 1930

Wanakaza win
(Old Lady Behavior Woman)
1890 - 1980

Wihopa
(Pretty Woman)
1910 - 2000

INTRODUCTION

Wihopa (Agnes Ross), a Mdewakanton, was born in 1910 on her father's farm at Flandreau, South Dakota.

The Mdewakantonwan are one of seven tribes.
The original seven tribes are known as Oceti Sakowin (seven campfires). Today these seven tribes are more commonly known as Sioux. (The word Sioux is a french corruption of an Ojibwa word meaning enemy.) The individual tribes are called:

- *Mdewakantonwan (Spirit Water Dwellers)*
- *Sissetonwan (Fish Scale Dwellers)*
- *Wahpetonwan (Camp Among the Leaves Dwellers)*
- *Wahpekute (Shoots Through the Leaves Dwellers)*
- *Ihanktonwan (End Dwellers)*
- *Ihanktonwana (Little End Dwellers)*
- *Titonwan (Prairie Dwellers)*

The first four tribes are known collectively as the Santee. They lived primarily on the Minnesota and Mississippi Rivers in what is now the state of Minnesota.

The Ihanktonwan and Ihanktonwana lived in eastern and southeastern part of what is called South Dakota today.

The Titonwan tribe has seven bands called Oglala (Scatter One's Own), Sicangu (Burnt Thigh), Miniconju (Plant by Water), Itazipco (No Bows), Ohenupa (Two Kettle), Sihasapa (Black Foot), and Hunkpapa (Camp at Entrance). These seven bands lived primarily in western North Dakota, South Dakota, Nebraska, eastern Wyoming, and in southeastern Montana.

The language of the seven tribes has three different dialects. The Santee group speaks Dakota, the Ihanktonwan group speaks Nakota, and the Titowan speak Lakota.

The original nation, the Oceti Sakowin (Seven Campfires), believed their origins were from Wicahpi Sakowin (Seven Stars of the Pleiades).

Wihopa was born and raised in an era in which

oil lamps were used for light, because they had no electricity. They would pump water out of a well and haul it into the house, because they didn't have plumbing in the house. Travel was by horse and wagon, because most people could not afford an automobile -- besides highways were few and far between. As a matter of fact, the world's first highway wasn't built until 1921 and it was in Germany! A few people owned a battery radio. These early radios utilized an antenna. The antenna was usually attached to the house and connected to the nearest tree. There were no televisions, because TV was not invented until 1926. In the winter, the home was heated by wood and, if one could afford it, coal. People literally buttoned up for the winter weather, because the zipper was not introduced until 1914 and flu antibiotics were not discovered until 1928. Then, to make matters worse, the stock market collapsed in 1929, making it hard for wage workers to earn money. Even if you had money, goods and supplies were limited. Country people usually fared better during the Depression, because they could grow vegetables and fruits which would then be canned to eat during the winter time. The reason I mention these things is because I would like people to understand why my mother has strong beliefs about being conservative and thrifty; also for the youth of today to realize that they shouldn't take modern conveniences for granted. People should take time to appreciate what they have.

Wihopa was raised in an era in which she lived through five world wars: World War I to the Gulf War. She has lived through 16 Presidents of the United States: President Taft to President Clinton. Wihopa was fortunate enough to get a college education. She graduated in 1938 with a teaching degree. She retired from the Bureau of Indian Affairs in 1972 after 34 years of service. A majority of those years were spent teaching on the Rosebud and Pine Ridge Reservations in South Dakota. At the time my mother was born, the Sioux of South Dakota were still reminiscing about the Battle of the Little Big Horn, which was a mere 34 years before her birth. Traditionally, warriors were allowed to boast about their Brave Deeds . This book is my mothers Boast Book . In her waning years, it is acceptable to brag about her life's accomplishments. A majority of her life has been dedicated to the education of American Indian Youth. Even after her retirement, she taught as a contract teacher at Flandreau Indian School for several years. The remainder of her retirement has been as a Tribal Chairperson and educational consultant to schools, universities, and the State of South Dakota.

Wihopa is now the oldest living member of the Flandreau Santee Sioux Tribe and, as the keeper of the female medicine bundle, she is also the Sun Dance Grandmother for the Black Hills Sun Dance.

The format of this book has been divided into three sections. Section One is an interview of Wihopa (Agnes Ross) by Susan Koyama. Ms. Koyama is a student of American Indian History and the author of several Japanese language books on American Indians. Ms. Koyama originally comes from Fuji, Japan, and currently resides in Denver, Colorado. Section Two is comprised of memories of their mother by Allen, Kenneth, Duane, and James Ross compared to Wihopa's Astro-map interpretations. The reason for this comparison is to show the validity of astrology and the very real possibility of using astrology as a counseling tool. Section Three is an analysis of a female medicine bundle connection to the Feminine Energy. As you read this book, it is the hope of my mother that the information gleaned be used to help people understand each other.

WIHOPA

1938

1998

INTERVIEW OF WIHOPA (AGNES ROSS)

Interviewer: I have no format or questions that I plan to ask you. I will record anything you have to say and Dr. A.C. Ross will transcribe the tapes and organize the material into a book. Dr. Ross tells me you were born in 1910. So, you would be 88 years old.

Mother: You know, I am now the oldest living member of my Tribe.

Interviewer: What is the name of your Tribe?

Mother: Mdewakanton - translated into English it means Spirit Water People.

Interviewer: I was born in 1941. I only hope I will be in as good a physical condition as you when I reach your age.

Mother:	Thank you.
Mother:	My second son, Kenneth, attended the University of Minnesota. The university sent him educational materials. I came across an article among these materials that I agreed with very much, because it pertains to women. The article stated that physical activity is good for girls.

I can remember as a young girl, I was the fastest runner in the whole Flandreau community. During the 4th of July celebrations, they had foot races. They'd give you a dime if you won the race. A dime was a large amount of money in those days. I'd win every time, because I was so fast. As I grew up, I was a good basketball player, a good tennis player and when I went to the Northern Arizona University at Flagstaff, Arizona, my female classmates invited me to join the Delta Kappa Gamma Society -- a women's sorority in physical education. I was very naive and I didn't know very much about it, so I said OK. About a week later, the girls came back and told me that I couldn't join. The Director came to me and said, "I'm

4th of July - 1930

Front Row: 2nd from left (boy on one knee) - Charlie Allen; (4 boys sitting on ground) 1st boy on left - Vern Allen; 3rd boy from left - Kenny Allen; behind left shoulder on Vern is Margaret Allen; behind Kenny is Martha (Mary) Standing Cloud. Middle Row: 2nd from right side (standing)- John Allen. Back Row: 1st woman from right side - Clara Allen; 2nd woman from right side - Ida Allen; in front of Ida Allen is Dorothy Allen sorry, but according to the constitution of the organization, the organization is for Caucasians only." This is one of the times I came upon discrimination. That was in the 1938. I said it was all right, but the girls felt bad. They petitioned to have that stricken from the constitution. So, in 1939, my senior year at N.A.U., I was accepted in. Then I was told that it cost to join the organization. They all chipped in the money for the entrance fee -- I think it was $25.00. So the girls helped me to get into the organization. I have the pin and the certificates.

People ask if I've ever been discriminated against. I say, "Yes, but I don't let it bother me." I had a Physical Education minor, along with my major in Elementary Education. When I started my teaching career, I was given a job as a Recreational Aide in a Government Indian School in Hayward, Wisconsin. They had programs where you work for the students. It was a lot of fun and I enjoyed it, but you have to start young to do things like that. People don't believe I'm that old because I can still do the Macarena. Just teasing.

Interviewer: What do you think about the Crazy Horse mountain?

Mother: I think it's good to educate people that come from all over the world. They say it's good; they're honoring him. But some Indian people feel it's desecrating the mountain. I suppose each one has their own viewpoint. I think it's nice, because it provides jobs for Indian people. I hope to see it finished. It's been taking so long.

I worked in the Black Hills, in the summer of 1930, at a place called Sylvan Lake Hotel. We used to sit alongside the lake. The hotel I worked in burned down. I earned one dollar a day as a waitress. During the Depression days, a dollar a day was a lot of money.

Interviewer: Were you living in that area?

Mother: No, I went to Sylvan Lake from Haskell Institute, Haskell is a school for American Indians. There were about 10 of us girls who went to Sylvan Lake from Haskell. Haskell is in Lawrence, Kansas; it's a four year college now.

5

SYLVAN LAKE GIRLS
Agnes - front left

Interviewer: Some people believe that Chief Crazy Horse gave an order to never have his picture taken.

Mother: Well, a lot of the old time Indians did not want their pictures taken. They said it robbed you of your spirit, it took

6

something from you. In those days, pictures were not hung all over like we do today. I do know that in the old days, a lot of Indians, like Crazy Horse, didn't want their photo taken.

They don't even know where Crazy Horse is buried. I have a grandfather named Wowinape. When he died, his wife took him and buried him. No one knows where he's buried. When we travel to Minnesota, where my people originally came from, we know that his body is there, but we don't know exactly where. In the olden days, that's the way it was. They didn't advertise, "Well, we're going to bury you here and put up a big monument."

Last night we watched a television program about Sri Lanka, which is an island off India. The title of the program was Sacred Stones. It showed where those people used to carve on the rocks in the caves where they found shelter. These carvings are similar to American Indian carvings. I think all people, whether they were American Indian or not, have their own ways of doing things that are similar to other groups.

Interviewer: Let me tell you some similarities with Indian culture to the Japanese people. Talking about the picture thing. In Crazy Horse's time, that is about the same time that the first Americans went to my homeland. They went there because they needed cork for their fishing business; they needed cork for supplies. At this time, people responded just the same way as you described. The Japanese said when you stand before the camera it would suck up your spirit, so your spirit isn't seen. So don't let them take your picture.

Mother: You wonder what they were thinking. A camera, I imagine, was mysterious to them. They didn't know what was going to happen. They always said, Oh, don't take my picture, you'll steal my spirit.

We had a Japanese friend, she graduated from Chadron State in Nebraska. She never did say why she came over to the States to go to school. I think some of her relatives were living around Chadron during World War II. They had removed a lot of Japanese from the coast and moved them to places in Nebraska and Wyoming -- Japanese internment camps; I think some of her people were there. That's where she came from. Anyway, she graduated from Chadron State and was looking for a teaching job. I was a teacher's supervisor on the Pine Ridge Reservation. I signed her up to work for me. She was with me for about five years and then she decided to go into a different government school program overseas. I still hear from her.

Her parents invited us to Hawaii and they were just wonderful to us. They kept us for a whole week; then they flew us to Maui. She had an aunt that worked for the U.S. Federal Government; she was a nurse in Maui. I have a lot of pictures of the family and Jeannie still teaches in Germany. Jeannie Tsue. That was her maiden name, now her name is Jeannie Grines. She's married and they have one son. I think their son graduated from high school this year. They're closing down all the overseas base schools and she wants to get back into the Bureau of Indian Affairs Service in the States. She has asked me to help her. I told her that the Bureau of Indian Affairs schools are changing; the schools are being contracted to the tribes. So, maybe she won't be eligible. She might have to go back to Honolulu. She'd like to put in more years with the U.S. Federal Government, because she's got 25 years or more in with them. She could retire at 30 years.

Interviewer: Is Jeannie from Hawaii?

Mother: She is Hawaiian/Japanese. She has Japanese ancestry.

Interviewer: The reason I'm asking is that most of those people of Japanese ancestry who were sent to the internment camp during World War II are mostly from the west coast and very seldom from Hawaii.

Mother: She had relatives in Hawaii. I suppose they move around too. It sounded like they worked for the U.S. government over in Hawaii. The father worked for a shipping company; the mother worked in an office.

She took us to her office. She had coached the stenographers in how to say hello in the Dakota language. When she introduced us, the people all stood up and waved saying, "Hau! Hau!" That's a greeting in Dakota. We had a real good time for those two weeks.

Mother: I've been looking for a certain picture. It's a picture of a ship that took me to Europe way back in 1938. I was nominated to represent the Native Americans at a world conference of Christian youth held in Amsterdam, Holland. I went over seas -- everything was planned for me; all I had to do was follow directions. I traveled on the Holland-American Line. Every now and then I hear about the Holland-American Line. The name of the ship was the Rotterdam. I think it was torpedoed in World War II by the Germans. I think they destroyed it or crippled it or something.

I went from here to New York and then went across the bay where the Statue of Liberty stands. We passed right over to the New Jersey side to get to the ship. It took about a week to cross the Atlantic Ocean. That was before airplanes were so popular. It was before World War II started. I sometimes wonder -- well, didn't I have any sense to realize how hazardous it might have been?

Christian Delegation to Europe
(Agnes - Front Row, 5th from left)

We got to London and then crossed the English Channel to Amsterdam. The convention lasted about a week. I was sponsored by the Young Women's Christian Association. There was another Young Women's Christian Association convention in Brussels, Belgium following this convention; there I met some more Young Women's Christian Association girls. Following that, the U.S. government wanted me to go to Elsinore, Denmark, to the People's International College, to attend a workshop on how cooperatives were formed. This was because the U.S. government was trying to get the Indians started in cooperatives, all different kinds of activities like that. Over there, at that time, all the travel was by train. So, from Brussels, I went to Berlin, Germany on the train.

Interviewer: Did you see any signs of the Nazi's?

Mother: Oh, all kinds of signs. The soldiers or police, whatever they were, they all wore swastikas on their arms and were all over the place, but that didn't bother me. A couple of Norwegian girls were with me; they were going home to Norway. We saw the stadium where the 1936 Olympics were held. We toured all over the place, looking at buildings, then we took off to visit Hamburg, Germany. We had to get off the train to get on to a ship that would take us up to Denmark. You'd think that when you got on the train you'd show your tickets, but there they wanted to see our tickets as we got off. I showed my tickets and that conductor or whatever he was took my tickets, tore them up, and dropped them into the wastebasket. Now, I was stranded. I couldn't go anywhere without my tickets.

Interviewer: Why did he destroy your tickets?

Mother: The two Norwegian girls were just horrified. The girls told me to stand there over the wastebasket. Just down the hallway was the American Consulate; they told them what happened to me. As I stood there, it was no time at all that a man from the American Consulate came down the street and made that man pick up the pieces and make new tickets for me. You know why they did that? Because he thought I was Jewish. That was just the time that they were gathering all the Jews. I might have been mistaken as one of them; so these girls saved my life. We went on to Elsinore, Denmark, and they went on home.

Agnes and Norwegian girl

The college made a tour across Sweden. Heaven knows how I got back to Amsterdam. I don't know how in the world I managed all that, but I did. That's another time I was involved in discrimination. Because somebody saw that I was a minority race.

Interviewer: Were you the only Indian person?

Mother:	Yes, I was the only one.
	We have a niece, Virginia Driving Hawk, that married a Norwegian named Vance Sneve. He was telling my husband, Harvey, "You know after I die, I hope that I come back. If I am reincarnated, I want to come back as an Indian. They have so many good cultural values."
Interviewer:	So tell me about the Indian belief system.
Harvey:	The traditional Indians have a belief that says when you die your spirit goes to the Milky Way. There an old woman sits and, if you've fulfilled your mission on earth, she passes you on and you go on the Milky Way to the spirit world. If she doesn't, you come back to earth to fulfill your mission.
Interviewer:	So, if you are not a complete being, you are still not finished or qualified to enter the spirit world, you have to come back over and over again.
Harvey:	Yes, to complete your evolutionary journey.

16

Interviewer: You have so many turtles around, why?

Harvey: A turtle is a symbol of a long life. They are hard to kill.

Interviewer: Harvey is right. One day we cut a turtle into pieces and the heart was still pounding.

Harvey: We butchered one once. They tell the story that if you swallow the live heart you would be brave. So we did -- we swallowed the heart and it was beating when we did this.

Interviewer: Why does the turtle mean so much to you?

Mother: It's a symbol that we believe in. Originally, the turtle, especially the ocean turtles, survived for 100's of years. The turtles found in the desert survive without any water. They live a long life. I don't know when I started collecting turtles. But it seems like everybody just fell into that routine of giving me turtles. I'm going to show you a turtle that I got from a Filipino lady named Dina. She

17

married my nephew, Dick Allen. They lived in Los Angeles, California. When her mother-in-law passed away, Dina came here for the funeral and visited our Indian cemetery. Later, when she got cancer, she told her husband, Dick, that this is where she wanted to be buried. So, when she passed away, they brought her here to bury her. The last time she was here she gave me this turtle. She's with us now.

Interviewer: This is another similarity, Japanese believe the turtle is a sign of longevity. The crane and the turtle are two symbols of longevity and health.

Mother: Last week we had a grandson come. He said, "Grandpa, I have something for you in the pick-up truck." We went out there and he had a turtle in his pick-up. Grandpa said, "We'll let it go down here in the creek, because they come out of the water this time of year to lay eggs." It is during this time that the roads have a lot of turtles on them. When the wild roses bloom in Spring, the turtles come out to lay their eggs. When we went out to the pick-up truck, the turtle had already begun to lay its eggs. We had to hurry and get it to the creek or someplace where it could bury the eggs.

Harvey: She asked you about cultural beliefs. Why don't you tell her about our Grandson David killing his first deer?

Mother: Oh yes, our grandson came here. He had gotten a new gun for Christmas in 1995 and he was so proud of it. He went deer hunting and got his first deer. His dad helped him carry it and they brought it here to the garage. Grandpa had to help him -- show him how to skin it and cut it up. He said, "OK, Grandpa, I've got it all cut up." Harvey said, "OK, wrap up each piece and give it away -- that's an old Indian tradition." On your first kill you share it with others, especially the elderly. So his dad helped him pedal all these packages of deer meat to all the elderly on the reservation. He gave it all away because that was tradition. That's the sharing part. You share your first kill with those that are needy or elders.

Interviewer: Tell us about your elementary school days.

Mother: Spafford. That was the name of our elementary school. The first school that I attended burned down when I was in the sixth grade. Then we had to hold classes at the bank and in different churches until they built Spafford. My class was the first class to graduate from Spafford.

Interviewer: You graduated elementary when you were fourteen years of age?

Mother: Yes, but my older sister, Clara, was not happy in elementary school. She cried all the time and would run away. They had a hard time keeping her in school. So the principal said, "Well, start sending Agnes with her, then she will have someone to communicate with, someone to be with her." So, I started school early. We both had to learn English together because we spoke only Dakota.

Interviewer: Did you have a hard time learning English?

Mother: Not that I recall. But again, I experienced
               discrimination. There were some little
               boys in our class who used to poke fun at
               us. They would say things about us, but
               I never did pay much attention. My
               brother used to fight when somebody
               teased him, but I didn't let what people
               said bother me. I didn't hit them, or chase
               them, or whatever they wanted me to do.
               I didn't do it.

Interviewer: Did you go to the Flandreau Indian
               School?

Mother: Yes. One year my mother worked up here
               for the Flandreau Indian School. She
               taught weaving. Our high school
               downtown didn't teach Home-Economics.
               That's all the school went to was the tenth
               grade and my mother wanted me to come
               and take Home-Economics, because it was
               kind of a vocational school. So, I came to
               school for one year and learned how to
               use a sewing machine and learned how to
               use an electric or gas stove, whatever it
               was. Out where we lived we just had
               wood stoves and oil lamps. We had to fire
               up the wood stove. It was different and

she wanted me to learn the modern mechanical things. I came up here one year and graduated tenth grade.

**Haskell Graduation
1931**

Then I went back to Flandreau Public High School until I graduated. My sister, Clara, went on to Haskell School, in Lawrence, Kansas, right after she finished Flandreau Indian School. Later I went to Haskell and graduated with my two year teaching degree.

Interviewer: You just told me something that struck my attention. You told me that your mother taught weaving.

Mother: Well, yes. The government made looms.
              They were not like the Navaho looms.
              The government looms were machines. I
              don't know how you do it, but it was used
              to weave rugs and blankets.

Interviewer: So you mean these are not the traditional
              looms?

Mother: Yes, weaving belongs to southwest people.
              They built looms upright and did the
              weaving by hand. They raised sheep and
              made their own wool.

Interviewer: That sounds weird to me. Sounds like
              they tried to make Navaho's out of the
              students.

Mother: Well, you know how the government is.
              They tried to make us farmers and most
              Indian people didn't farm. They tried to
              force things on us like co-operatives.
              They made people study co-operatives
              and tried to form co-operatives among
              the Indian people, but it didn't work out.
              A few reservations had turkey co-oper-
              atives, but the turkeys went wild out there
              on the prairie.

Interviewer: Turkey farms?

Mother: Turkeys are trained to come home to roost at a certain place, but it just fizzled out.

Interviewer: I don't think it would work.

Mother: No, it didn't work. And they tried to have cattle co-operatives, where two or three families went together and pooled their cattle and raised them. It didn't work out either.

Interviewer: So, Spafford Elementary School was not a Bureau of Indian Affairs school or church school?

Mother: No, it was a public school.

Interviewer: Were you born on the reservation in Flandreau?

Mother: Yes. First, let me explain how our reservation came into existence. The following is taken from my son's book Ehanamani.

"In 1851, my ancestors, the Santee Sioux, signed a

24

treaty with the United States government relinquishing 24 million acres in southern Minnesota for $3 million. As a part of the payment for the lands, my ancestors were promised farm equipment, farm animals, teachers, and health care.

In 1854, several Santee were murdered by a white whiskey seller. This prompted a hatred for white people by their leader, Inkpaduta. Then, in the winter of 1857, one of Inkpaduta's Santee killed a dog that had bitten him. The owner and other whites forcibly disarmed the Santee. Hungry and unable to hunt for food, they rearmed themselves and took revenge by killing over 40 people in three different incidents.

SANTEE SIOUX TREATIES

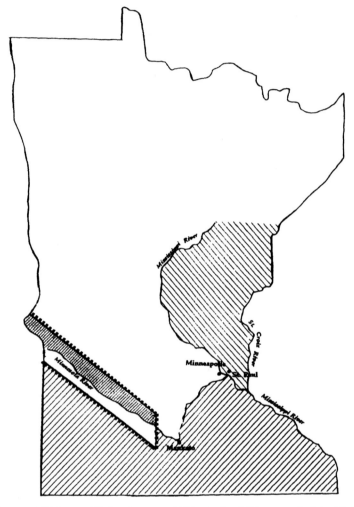

Treaty 1837: All land east of Mississippi River ceded to United States Government.

Treaty 1851: 24 million acres ceded to the United States Government.

Santee Sioux land as of the 1851 Treaty: 10 miles north and 10 miles south of Minnesota River by 140 miles long. (Map area outlined with bold dashed line.)

Treaty 1858: All land north of Minnesota River ceded to the United States Government.

Eight Week War of 1862: All remaining land lost.

By 1858, 150,000 Europeans had settled in southern Minnesota. My ancestors had relocated to an area 140 miles long and 20 miles wide on both sides of the Minnesota River. In 1858, the government negotiated a new treaty with our Santee people, in which the northern half of this reservation was relinquished, with promises of more money, farm equipment, farm animals, and teachers. In 1861, my ancestors' crops failed and they started moving out into what was their former reservation to hunt. This was against the law, stated the government agents. The agents kept warning my ancestors to stay on the reservation. In 1862, our crops failed again. So we went to the agency for help, and asked when our money from the U.S. government would arrive to help our people through the hard winters.

Much of our money had gone to traders in the past, because when we needed supplies and goods, we had gone to the traders and bought them on credit. Then when the money came in from the government, the traders would ask the agents to pay the debt. The debt was usually over and above what was actually purchased by our people.

Finally, in August of 1862, my Santee ancestors became frustrated because of the lack of help. They went to the government agent and the agent said, "I'll leave it up to the traders." "What do you traders think?" he asked.

One said, "You Sioux could eat grass for all I care."

The traders wouldn't give the people any help, so 400 Santees surrounded the agency and went into the storage cabins and took what they could carry. Still, this was not enough for the entire tribe.

In the meantime, roving bands of our hungry people started to raid the settlers for food. In one incident, they ended up fighting and killing some settlers. With that, our chiefs called a council to decide what to do.

Little Crow, Chief of our people, said, "No, no, we must not fight. There are too many; they are too strong." The young men called him a coward.

He replied, "No, I'm not a coward. I have been to Washington, D.C. I rode on the train many days and each morning I woke up and I saw more and more white men. There's no way you will win this war." He continued, "I'm not a coward; I will fight with you and I will die with you."

Thus, a series of seven battles took place. They were started by my Santee ancestors against the U.S. soldiers and surrounding towns. Reinforcements arrived and the last two battles were won by the soldiers, who now outnumbered the Santees two to one. The soldiers had cannons, which turned the tide in the battles and brought an end to the eight-week war. This was called a war, not a rebellion, because American Indians were not U.S. citizens until 1924 and were not allowed to vote until 1948.

Four thousand Santees packed up and went west and north into Canada. Those who went west, included Inkpaduta and a small group of Santee who eventually fought in the Battle of the Little Big Horn. Those who went north, did so for protection under the British, since the Santee were allies to the British against the Americans in the War of 1812. The remaining Santees, approximately 2,000 -- most of them women and children, were force-marched to prison at Fort Snelling. They formed a four mile-long procession in this march. Along the way, the settlers stoned, clubbed, and stabbed the people with pitchforks. After a month of trials, the U.S. government sentenced 303 of the 2,000 to hang. President Lincoln reviewed the trial records and reduced this number to 38. Thirty-eight Santee men where hung on December 26, 1862 in a mass hanging at Mankato, Minnesota. The largest mass hanging in the history of the United States. The remaining 1,700 Santees were placed in the compound at Fort Snelling and lived that winter camped out in the cold. My people lacked sufficient firewood and food and 300 died at Fort Snelling that winter from the cold and sickness. The rest of the survivors were loaded onto cattle barges and towed down the Mississippi River and then up the Missouri River to Fort Thompson, South Dakota. There my ancestors remained for three years.

While at Ft. Thompson, our crops failed again and the people wanted to go home.

The government moved them to a reservation in northeastern Nebraska. Many were still homesick and wanted to go back to Minnesota. The federal government finally stated that the Santees could return to their homelands only if they homesteaded the land like any other U.S. citizen. So twenty-five Santee families did exactly that. They left Nebraska and started for our homeland in Minnesota.

The Homestead Act was passed in the spring of 1862, and much of our Santee homeland was now occupied by settlers who had come mainly from northern Europe. The twenty-five families reached an area along the Big Sioux River that had not been homesteaded, in what was then called Dakota Territory.

C.K. Howard set up a trading post among our people who had homesteaded on the Big Sioux River. The first townsite was named after Charles Flandreau.

The Mdewakanton Santee of Flandreau organized and became recognized as a tribe under the 1934 Indian Reorganization Act. Today, there are approximately 500 Santees on the Flandreau Santee Sioux Tribal Role; but because of lack of employment on the reservation, fewer than a hundred of us actually live on the Flandreau Santee Sioux Reservation.

They came this far and they settled along the river."

Interviewer: The Big Sioux River?

Mother: Yes, the Big Sioux and it has the Dakota name Wakpa Ipaksan (Bend in the River). That's what they call Flandreau Indian community today.   At the bend of the river, that is where we camped.   The government took over all the land and opened it for homesteads.   The white people came in and took what they wanted.

Interviewer: Was that after that Minnesota war?

Mother: After the Minnesota fighting, they tried to move all of the Santee out of Minnesota. Twenty-five families wanted to stay here. So my Grandmother, Martha (Mary) Standing Cloud, with her two sisters, took out homesteads.   Our grandma's homestead was down here on the river. She took out a homestead and they had to pay $12.00 for the application.   These twenty-five families got their homesteads all along the bend of the river. They had to abide by the Homestead Act.   The Homestead Act says you have to fence, you have to plant trees, you have to till the soil -- you have to do this, you have to do that. All sorts of things.

Grandma Martha Standing Cloud

Standing (L-R): Alex Wakeman, Chris Heminger, Felix Heminger
Seated (L-R): Tom Heminger, Grandma Standing Cloud, Wesley Heminger

Some of the things they could comply
with, but the other things they couldn't.
At the end of 10 years, the land became
taxable. People didn't have the money to
pay taxes. People didn't have farm
animals or equipment to till the soil like
they were supposed to. So, gradually,
they sold out to the white people. The
white people bought the Indian land, but

my Grandmother held on to her assignment. My father was 8 or 9 years old at that time. He grew up to be a good farmer. He learned the regulations and paid the taxes so, we saved the land.

Interviewer: The government didn't pay attention to the fact that you are Indian not white?

Mother: No, because my dad paid the taxes and did everything he was supposed to do. We kids came along and there were so many of us, nine in the family. We did most of the chores around the house or farmstead, because he was usually out in the hay field or cultivating or whatever had to be done. We kids took care of the cows, we brought them in and milked them. We raised chickens; sold the eggs; and sold the milk and the cream -- those kinds of things to help out. We kids did a lot of the work.

Interviewer: So answer me a question. Before your grandmother's time, your people were hunters and didn't know anything about modern farming. How did your grandmother learn farming?

Mother: Originally we farmed, but it was small, more like gardening. Now, we had to have the animals to farm with; then you just copied the white people and did it.

John Allen on farm.

Then you got hold of a horse and you would have to harness it. My dad was very good with horses. Well, I'll tell you, he was half white -- he was born illegitimate. His father was an Army officer from St. Louis and was stationed at Ft. Sioux Falls. I think that he kind of helped us and supported my Dad by getting a horse for him. My dad did the farming. I tell the kids nowadays when I talk to them, that they don't know how fortunate they are. I said, You come to school, the bus stops outside your door, and you get on and ride to school. When I was young, I had to walk to school. I did all my chores, then I had to hike down the road 2 1/2 miles to go to school. Rain or shine or snow, no matter what the weather, that was what we had to do. Nowadays, kids come to school and at noon they serve them a hot lunch right in the school building. In those days, when I went to school, there was no such thing as a hot lunch. If Mom had bread or biscuits, you stuck it in a paper sack and you brown bagged it to school. That is what you ate when it came lunch time.

Interviewer: When I was walking, I walked by the Indian cemetery. I found Chief Little Crow's monument. Do you care to tell me anything about Chief Little Crow?

Mother: I don't know too much about him, that was before my time. My grandfather, Wowinape, my mom's dad, is the son of Little Crow. Like I told you, we don't

SOUTH DAKOTA DEPARTMENT OF HEALTH
DIVISION OF VITAL STATISTICS
DELAYED CERTIFICATE OF BIRTH

State File No. _____
Co. Reg. No. 11512

Full Name at Birth Ida Cora Wakeman   Date of Birth April 1, 1891   Sex Female

Birthplace Rosebud Twp   Mody   South Dakota   Color, Color. Indian
(City or Town)   (County)   (State)

Father: Full Name Thomas Wakeman   Age _____   Birth- Place Minnesota
(State or Country)

Mother: Maiden Name Judith (David Faril)   Age _____   Birth- Place Minnesota
(State or Country)

Affidavit: I hereby declare upon oath that the above statements are true.

Signature Ida Wakeman Allen   Address Flandreau, S.D.
(To be signed by informant)

Subscribed and sworn to before me this 19th **day of** March, 1956

SEAL Eugene Laird Clerk Court Notary Public

ABSTRACT OF SUPPORTING EVIDENCE Mody C.J. Dak.

1. Affidavit of Parentage Nov 19-1956   April 1891 South Dakota
2. Own child birth Cert # 9074   7-9-1925   age 34 yrs South Dakota
3. Own child birth Cert # 9075   7-6-1927   age 36 yrs South Dakota

---

I hereby certify that the abstract of evidence above recorded is to my knowledge true and correct.

Signature Eugene Laird   Date signed March 8, 1956
Clerk of Courts Mody C. J. Dak   Registrar Eugene Laird
(Title of Reviewing Official)

Date Filed March 23, 1956

40

Wowinape changed his name to Thomas Wakeman. Birth certificate shows him as my mother's father.

even know where my grandfather is buried, because he didn't want his body to be mistreated like his father's, Little Crow. Little Crow's bones were hanging in a museum. When you learn stories like that about how the white people treated the remains of Indians, you get sick.

Wowinape (16 years old).
Photo taken while prisoner
at Ft. Snelling, MN - 1864.

Anyway, we don't know where my Grandpa Wowinape is buried. We know that his wife took him back to Minnesota, because that is what he wanted – to be buried in his original homeland.

Interviewer: Is there any site in Mankato, Minnesota that commemorates that mass execution?

Mother: Yes, they have ceremonies every year now, but I never attended one, so I don t know what they are like. All I know is we have the names of the men who were hung at our cemetery. At the entrance there is a white buffalo that lays in front of the big stone, but on the back side is the list of the 38 men hung; then down below are names of World War I veterans, World War II veterans, and now I see names of the Korean Veterans and the Vietnam Veterans.

Interviewer: People buried there are all your people?

Mother: Well, it's a mixture. We have two white people. I have a great-aunt, Annie Bauer, who married a German, his name was Uffie Bauer. He came from Germany. I don't know his status, if he ever became a citizen or not, but he was a real good farmer on their homestead. He used to farm their homestead for his wife, Annie. She passed away first and she's buried up there and he died later. In his will, he told his nephews that he wanted to be buried next to his wife. So we have a German up there in that cemetery. Then we have two missionary women that worked here for many, many years. One of them, Marjorie Hibbard, wanted to be buried there. She was from Buffalo, New York. Also, Dina, the Filipino girl wanted to be buried there. She's up there too.

Interviewer: So the cemetery out there is mostly for your people. Could you tell me why is that? Why it became your people's cemetery?

Mother: Well, the missionaries came and had the Indians build that church. It's the first church in this area; they call it the First Presbyterian Church. The church is over 100 years old.

Interviewer: Do they still hold services there?

Mother: Occasionally. They do have participants, but they can't afford to have a full time minister. They do have a nice reception building, which was built about 20 years ago. The thing is that we Indians can't afford to pay the utilities. If we could pay the utilities, we would have electric lights, running water, and modern flush toilets, but there is no way to pay for those fees. The tribe takes care of mowing the lawn and keeping it so it looks nice. A lot of people come through there to view the cemetery, because it's such an historical cemetery. Now, the headstones are falling apart, because they are so old.

Interviewer: Dr. A.C. Ross talked about Chief Little Crow in his book Ehanamani. So I know a little about him. Do you care to relate any story you know about his burial?

Mother: My mother said that shortly after she was married to my dad, they had gone to St. Paul, Minnesota. They came upon a museum; they went in and there hung the bones of her grandfather.

Interviewer: What year was that?

Mother: This was in the early 1900's. Anyway, these bones were hanging in the museum. When she came home and told her brother, Jessie, about it, he made a trip over there to see for himself. He went to the museum caretaker and said that he wanted those bones taken out or he would get the law or get someone to help him. I guess they did -- they took them down, boxed them up, and put them in the basement of the museum. It was several years later that my Uncle Jesse inquired about the remains. He got in touch with an historian out of St. Paul and they found out that the box of remains was in the basement of the museum. So, he's the one that went through the legal procedure of getting them returned. They brought them over here and the burial took place here in 1972. That was 109 years after he died. The following is taken from my son's book Ehanamani.

"In 1972, Little Crow, who was the Chief of the Mdewakanton Santee during the eight-week war in Minnesota, was finally buried at Flandreau, South Dakota. He was killed in 1863, and he was buried in 1972 -- 109 years after he was killed. When he was killed, his remains were put on display at the State Capital in Minnesota. Eventually, they ended up with the State Historical Society. My great-uncle, Jessie Wakeman, my mother's uncle, was the grandson of Little Crow. He had tried for years and years to get the remains returned, but to no avail. It was in 1972 that a friend of mine named David Beaulieu, whom I had met at the University of Minnesota when I was attending school there, was working for WCCO, a television station in Minneapolis. David and the station began a documentary on Little Crow. They were going to expose the State Historical Society of Minnesota for not releasing Little Crow's remains to his relatives. As soon as the Historical Society found out about the documentary, they agreed to give the remains to Uncle Jessie; also agreeing to transport the remains to Flandreau, and pay for the monument for his grave site. Fewer than ten people went to the burial, held in September of 1972. Uncle Jessie was there, and my grandma and my mother. Shortly after that, Uncle Jessie died. I guess he was just waiting to get the remains of Little Crow returned and buried. Once that was accomplished, he went on to the spirit world himself. On the gravestone of Little Crow was engraved his Indian name, "Ta-Oyate Duta" (His Red People) and the following: "Therefore, I will die with you."

LITTLE CROW (Ta Oyate Duta)
Photo taken during Mdewakanton and Wahpekute
delegation trip to Washington, DC in 1858.

Mother: Then the following year we had a real
           nice memorial service. I was the Tribal
           chairperson then, so I organized a
           program, got a speaker to read the
           service, and I got the Indian school choir
           to sing spiritual hymns. It was a real nice
           service.

When they brought the remains back in 1972, my uncle didn't want anyone to know about it. He wanted everything to be hush hush and quiet, and only the family to attend; because, at that time, there was a story going on about people fighting over Chief Sitting Bull's bones up on the Standing Rock Reservation. Some tribal members wanted him to be buried on their side of the river and the other people went over there, dug up the remains, stole them, and took them back. My Uncle Jessie didn't want that to happen with his grandfather Little Crow's remains, so he wanted to do everything quiet. They cemented the box into the ground and then the historical society helped put up that monument that is there. On the bottom of the monument is an etching "Therefore, I will die with you." We're proud of that. I was the one that had it put on there, because my uncle said he gave a famous speech to his people when they were accusing him of being a coward. Little Crow told them he was not a coward. He said, "I will fight with you and; therefore, I will die with you." So the historian had me write that in Dakota and they put it on his stone.

49

Interviewer: Why is there food placed at the grave site?

Mother: Because we Dakota believe in helping one's spirit after death, we brought all this corn and squash and everything to the grave site. The whole grave site is covered with food offerings which are to help the spirit on its journey. The next year is when we had a memorial ceremony and they had the four direction flags and the Indian school took part during the memorial ceremony.

Next time you go by there, notice the tomb honoring the veterans. We did that more recently. Harvey instigated that because he's a V.F.W. and on the Pine Ridge we were American Legion. So we were always taking care of the veterans part of things and they decided to put on a memorial and give away. Harvey saw to it that we had the white buffalo there at the cemetery. It is in the form of a circle. When they dedicated it, my son, Chuck, was the main speaker because he served in the military too.

Interviewer: We Japanese believe in prayers for our ancestors too. Do you still carry that war - rior tradition in this small community?

Mother:	Not like the old time Indians, but we do respect the veterans. I don't think many people carry on the real old traditional ways any longer. Out west they tried to say if you are the son of a chief then you can achieve title after he passes on, but that's not the traditional way. Traditionally, you had to earn the title. But they still honor their special veterans. I know that I had several first cousins, one was captured in Germany, and they asked him, "Why are you fighting for the Americans, when the Americans didn't treat you well at all?" He said, "I'm not fighting for them; I am fighting for my land, my country. That's my land."

Harvey didn't have to go to war. He was essential in the war industry. He worked for McDonnell Aircraft, he was married, had two children, and still he was dedicated enough to say, "I'm going, I want to go, I want to fight." So he enlisted in World War II. We had that patriotism in those days.

Harvey Ross (1946)
94th Infantry
General Patton's 3rd Army

Harvey had an uncle, Arthur Frazier, who
was killed in World War I. A couple of
years after this, his uncle walked into his
home. Here they said he was killed over
there and still he was alive. The government couldn't believe that it was the same
person. He had gone to school up here at
this Flandreau Indian School and had gone
with a group of men to enlist in the Army.
They brought him back here and said,
"Alright, this is where you went to school —
where is your room and where was your
class?" He went to the classroom and he
said, "This is where I used to sit."

His memory must have come back and he came home. Things like that happen. The government said, "Well, that's not him." They didn't want to recognize that they were wrong.

Interviewer: Tell me about Flandreau Indian School.

Mother: That's where I began taking an interest in teaching. My mother wanted me to get interested in Home-Economics, sewing, etc. I wasn't interested in it. I said I wanted to go into teacher education. They had a group of little kids at Flandreau Indian School -- we had to take care of them; we had to sleep with them in their dorm; we took them to school and took them to eat. We stayed with them most of the day. It was almost like baby-sitting, but I enjoyed working with them.

Interviewer: In your time, was Haskell Institute for Indian people only?

Mother: Yes, it was a U. S. government boarding school for Indians only.

Interviewer: I have heard a lot of bad things about the

Indian boarding schools compared to public schools. One time I asked an Indian person who was from the Pine Ridge Reservation, he was an educator. He said don't ask the people if they have good memory about it, because it is just another bad memory. They don't care to tell you about it. When I read books on it, nothing seems to tell you the way it was. Do you care to tell me anything about that. The positive side on the Indian Schools?

Mother: Some people say they are not as good as the public schools, but I think they were. I went there two years and I finished, then went on. My college accepted the credits from Haskell. We have some people who say that because they can't adjust. They were operated like military schools. You had to get up and make your bed, and be on time for everything. You lined up in companies, so many to a company. You had officers like the army. You had your lieutenants and you had your captains and all that. We had to wear uniforms, you couldn't wear your own clothes. You had to wear government issue clothes.

Interviewer: Were you the one's who had to maintain it?   I mean doing the laundry and mending and repairing the clothes.

Mother: Yes, the students did those things. They were detailed to work in the laundry, etc. The government had big machines called mangles that mangled your sheets and pillowcases.   Everything was military style when I was there. They are not that way now, I know. In recent years, I read about people complaining about the treatment they got at boarding schools. I think they were complaining about the Catholic schools.   The government assigned the churches to different reservations. Episcopal take care of this group, Catholics you go take care of those. I say I didn't know where I belonged when it came to organized religion; because, when I went to Haskell, I didn't know where the different denominations were.   My roommates were all Baptist, so I went to the Baptist church for a couple of years. When I went to N.A.U. in Flagstaff, the nearest church was across the street -- that was a Mormon Church, so I went to the Mormon church for a couple of years. I tell kids that I was like a spy, I went from one to another. But to me, religion is religion. You believe in God, he is there with you no matter where you are.

Interviewer: Back in those days, going in search of higher education was something that many people could not afford. Obviously, your parents were very dedicated to educate you or make sure you got a good education. How many of your people were able to afford to go to college?

Mother: Not very many.

Interviewer: So, how do you explain the fact that you went to college. I know that you are very brilliant and qualified; but, like you mentioned at the time, there were many racial barriers in those days, even today. Is that due to your parents' devotion for education?

Mother: They encouraged me. As far as financially, they couldn't help. When I first went out to work, I worked at Sylvan Lake for a dollar a day. I saved my dollar a day for the whole summer and I had

$100.00 to give to my father when he came after me at the end of the summer. Back then, $100.00 was a lot of money. It surprised him. He didn't know where to put it. We had an old Ford, it had rubber floor mats, and he took the money and stuck it under the rubber mat, so no one could find it.

Interviewer: Why didn't he take it to the bank?

Mother: He came to the Black Hills from Flandreau. After we returned, he probably put it in the bank in Flandreau. I worked and I always sent money home. In those days, Montgomery Wards and Sears Roebuck had catalogs. I would order things like oatmeal and things like that to be shipped home to my family. I just did it instinctively, it didn't hurt me to help. I had one brother, Kenneth, who graduated high school and he didn't have any nice clothes to wear when he was graduating, so I bought him a suit. It was just a way of being helpful. I always saved my money, so I could be prepared.

I was working in Hayward, Wisconsin when a teacher friend of mine said she was going to summer school, she said, "Come on Agnes, go to summer school with me." So I rode with her, paid my own tuition, and enjoyed that summer school. When we came back to work, I told her I was going to save my money to go back to school. She said, "Well, that's good." I came back and worked the fall semester. By December, I had saved my money and went back to college. At that time, we got a federal scholarship and it wasn't too much, $75.00 a year. Then this Young Women's Christian Association woman was interested in me and gave me a loan from the Indian Rights Association. She got me an education loan which I had to pay back after I got my degree, but I put myself through school by pinching pennies here and there. I worked for a college professor and his wife. I would go to their house on Saturdays to clean their house, do the laundry, or whatever had to be done. I think they only paid me a dollar for the work, but it was another dollar. I tell people about almost going barefooted, because the soles in my shoes had worn out. Every day I would have to take cardboard and lay the cardboard in the bottom of my shoes.

Interviewer: That must have been hard when it was wet?

Mother: Yes, but you get by.

Interviewer: You worked your way through college?

Mother: Yes, more or less. Two years at a time. Then when I started teaching at Pine Ridge Community School, I had to go back every three years to renew my teaching certificate. My supervisor said, "Agnes, why don't you take some requirements so you can get your masters." So I started taking my requirements. I went to school all day Saturdays at the state college in Chadron, Nebraska. I would teach all week and go to school on Saturdays, that way I earned my masters degree in Education.

Interviewer: Why did you work so hard?

Mother: I don't know. Just to keep myself busy. I didn't think the school work was hard.

Interviewer: You enjoyed it?

Mother: I enjoyed it. I enjoyed reading and writing. The only thing I didn't like was arithmetic. I have two published small books, one is about children's stories and the other is a collection of my poems.

Interviewer: Is this collection of poems written since your early times.

Mother: Quite a few of those I have written recently. I used to teach writing to the students. My supervisor sent one into the South Dakota State Department and it is in the State Poetry section. The State Book is called the Pasque , a spring flower. That one I know is in the Pasque. But some of these others I have written, they are in the centerfold. *The following is a poem by Agnes Ross.*

A FRIEND

Friends are persons who care
They help carry the burden.
Friends are those who share

They give everything and more.

A friendly word says a lot
To ease the pain of distress
A friendly touch of the hand
To reassure faith and confidence

A friend is there when needed
With just a quiet talk
A warm understanding smile
On a long, long lonely walk.

Be a friend, one who cares
Who is loving and understanding
Be a friend, one who shares
Who is giving and forgiving
Be a friend.

I think this is needed so much in today's living. Everybody talks about what do you do with these young kids that run wild. Well, they say it begins with the home. If you have parents that are caring and understanding, they can encourage kids to do better.

Interviewer: So, you teach Lakota language?

Mother: I have taught Lakota, but I am a Dakota
                speaker. A lot of people purchase my
                audio Dakota tapes for their own
                learning.

Interviewer: Today, people seem to have a lot of
                problems, because education is getting so
                bad.   School teachers have a lot of
                technical things like computers or engi-
                neering that they are good at, but there is
                something missing. What do you think
                about today's education?

Mother: I've been out of the classroom for 26 years,
                but I am still educating. When calculators
                came in, I said, "Do you think Indian kids
                out here on the reservation have a use for
                a calculator?"   They are not going to be
                out there in the field counting trees or
                counting sheep or counting cattle or
                counting whatever it is they have to
                count. They don't have a calculator to
                work it. I disapprove of calculators in the
                classroom. So many of them are depend-
                ent on calculators to figure out things for
                them nowadays. I don't think they think
                things out for themselves. I think they are
                too dependent on calculators.

I had a supervisor once that came into my classroom and she was just amazed at how I was teaching the little kids using the blackboard. I was telling them which words were verbs and which were adjectives. The simple way, you know, a verb is an action word, an adjective is descriptive word, and I was telling them. She said, "Agnes, if everybody taught the way you did, we wouldn't have any language problems."

Interviewer: So tell me, what is your philosophy of teaching? What is the most important thing in education?

Mother: Right now it is reading, because everything is written out; and, in order to learn, you have to read. On the other hand, if you use television or computers to tell you things, then I suppose television would be another way to learn.

Harvey and I sit here at nights watching television; we get absorbed in history about other countries that we haven't had the chance to read about. One time we saw where a group of warriors from

North Africa did something that pleased the people, and the women made the same tremolo noise that our people did when our warriors came home. Has it come down through the ages that the people have just sort of drifted apart? We sit there at night and watch stories on television, and like my son, Chuck, said when he was on maneuvers in Turkey, he came home and said those people have similarities to our people.

Interviewer: What do you mean by those people are like Indians?

Mother: He said those people have similar customs.

Interviewer: I agree that reading is very important even in this computer age, information comes on a screen, but kids still have to read it.

Mother: Yes, and, if you are not a fast reader, you don't finish the whole thing before it disappears.

Interviewer: That's always my problem, because English is my second language. I don't read that fast.

Mother: English is my second language too.

Interviewer: You said you teach the Lakota language.
               Why do you think it is so important to
               keep that language? Not many people
               even know it nowadays.

Mother: I know that is true, but do you know that
               the younger people are more interested in
               it now than ever before. They're the ones
               that are encouraging it. My kids say,
               Mom, why didn't you teach it to us when
               we were little? Because now they want to
               know the language. I taught the table
               grace to my grandson, so he can say the
               prayer in Dakota. Last summer at the Sun
               Dance they asked me to say grace. I took
               David up with me and asked David to say
               the grace for me; David prayed in Dakota.
               They were amazed that a youngster knew
               the Dakota prayer. I say that's when you
               need to teach it -- when they are young.

Interviewer: How do you explain that? Because young
               people are so bombarded with this main-
               stream culture nowadays?

Mother: We were talking about how to encourage the youngsters. This is a method I used to impress kids. Once we came in from recess into the classroom. We had a place to hang our coats. I came in last and noticed that all the coats were on the floor. So, I took off my coat and threw it into the floor too. The students all jumped up, everybody ran, grabbed their coats, and hung them up. That was a way to teach them without saying a word. I just took my coat off and threw it on the floor. I didn't have to say anything. You show them by example.

Interviewer: People don't do that nowadays.

Mother: No. If I see children doing something wrong, I will correct them. I say it must be the old teacher instinct, it's up to me to help correct them in situations or at least attempt to.

Interviewer: After you graduated from Northern Arizona University in 1938, you got a job at Pine Ridge for $45.00 a month for salary as a teacher apprentice. What is a teacher apprentice?

Mother: One might take this to be discriminatory, but back then, even if the Indian student graduated with a college degree, they could not go directly into a teaching position without proving to the federal government that they could teach. So I spent one year at Pine Ridge, and I had to prove myself.

Agnes Ross - N.A.U. graduation, 1938

In fact, the apprenticeship lasted for two years. There were several of us college graduates that were sent to Pine Ridge.

Each one of us was under a supervisory teacher. It's like taking practice teaching all over again. You help that teacher and you work with those kids in a specific area. You have to prove yourself for two years.

Interviewer: Even if you have a teacher certificate?

Mother: Even if you have your college degree, you couldn't go directly into the classroom, not in the Bureau of Indian Affairs at that time. I think it was because we were Indians. There were four of us girls and one boy. We had to prove ourselves there at Pine Ridge. I happened to be in the lowest teaching level. I helped in the bilingual situations. I worked with the little ones at the first grade level. At the end of the year, we were evaluated and my supervisor teacher said, "Agnes doesn't need another year of training." She recommended I be assigned to a teaching position. So I only served one year of apprenticeship. Then I came back to Rosebud Reservation, and the government assigned me to Horse Creek Day School. It was a two teacher school – eight grade levels. I had the first four grades and my classroom was in what they called the cannery. The cannery was under the Home Extension and that's where the local Indian people came to do their canning. They had community gardens and brought their fruits and vegetables there to do the canning. It sat vacant in the winter, so that is where they put me. I had my first four grades in the cannery while they were still working on the school building. It was about Christmas time when the new school building was ready for us to occupy. It was all brand new with desks and everything. The principal/teacher was Mr. Erickson. He had charge of the upper level, the 5, 6, 7 and 8 grades. I had almost 50 kids in my four grades, so I had to learn how to go from level to level. I did this by rotating the kids around. Besides teaching the classroom subjects, we had to supervise their weekly baths and do all those kinds of things to help out. We had a garden planted back behind the school building. During certain periods, they had to go out and pull weeds or cultivate their crops. In the spring of the year, I had a project which was probably unique in the schools at that time. Somewhere I got hold of an incubator and I got some fertilized eggs. We set the eggs in the incubator and had them in the classroom so the kids could see them hatching. Then I sponsored a 4H club with my students. When school closed in May, the little chicks were two or three months old and each one of the students took home some chicks to raise. I told them, if they wanted to, during the Rosebud Fair, they could bring their chickens back in for the fair. Some students won blue ribbons. The kids were going through the process of 4H work; they enjoyed that. That's one of the things we used to do and I enjoyed the garden part of it – being raised on a farm and knowing how to take care of things. Also, we had a couple of cows we had to milk. We had to show the kids how to bring the cows in, feed them, milk them, then bring the milk in. I was familiar with the farming process, because that was the way I was raised. The students had a lot of fun learning by doing.

Interviewer: Was it your invention, that curriculum.

Mother: No, it wasn't in the curriculum. I taught the way I thought they could learn best. What else are you going to do out there? You had to teach them something besides reading, writing, and arithmetic. We didn't have too many books to work with, so I had to improvise. I have always been a good singer, so I used to sing to the kids in the classroom; I would teach them songs. I would take a little Indian song and translate it into English. So, for English, they would go right into the English version of it. There was a man, he must have been a salesman or something, that came to listen to the kids singing, and he was so taken with the kids singing that he got us a set of music books for our school. He sent it to the school because we didn't have any music. I wasn't one to sit down and play the piano, so the principal's wife, who took care of the noon lunch, played the piano. I have some tapes where I have translated the music, I call it "Through Eden to Pine Ridge". She played the piano and I taught the music.

Interviewer: Teaching with music?

Mother: That was the way I taught the kids and they just enjoyed it. The Indian students could catch on to the new English words whether it was a little bit different from the Lakota or not, it didn't make any difference. They learned by doing and they enjoyed it. I did that even to the song "America". I put it in Lakota words and they would learn it in the Lakota and English language. They were learning two languages at the same time. Today it is called the whole brain method of learning.

Interviewer: How many children did you have in the same room?

Mother: I had 50 children in the same room. I would have to take the first grade reading class, while the others, maybe one group, were out taking care of the garden. The older kids helped the younger ones, because they weren't all six years old. The thing with beginners in those days was that some of your first graders were 11 or 12 years old. They had never attended school before; they only spoke Lakota and now they had a teacher who could help them -- because I was bilingual.

Interviewer: The age of all students ranged from 6 to 12 years old?

Mother: Yes, some of them were older than that.

Interviewer: Any kids you can tell me about?

Mother: There were two little white boys, one's father was a coach, the other's father was a guidance counselor at the boys dorm. They were sitting on the kindergarten table and some of the little boys were talking to each other in their Lakota language. One of the little white boys said, "Mrs. Ross, the boys are talking about us." So I said to those boys, "Well, what did you say?" The boys said this is what we said; we weren't talking about them. I had to explain to the white boys that the other boys speak another language and they were not talking about them. "Well," said the little white boy, "they are going to have to learn to speak my language too." I don't know what they were, German or Norwegian, but they felt bad that they were excluded and didn't have a language of their own to speak.

Interviewer: The language difference might have created some division for the children.

Mother: Well, that was the only time I detected there was something. The boys didn't understand what the little Lakota boys were saying, but they weren't, so they just went on. Nowadays, if some kids went off into a corner and talked a different language, one might say to one's self, "I wonder what they are talking about. Are they are talking about me." But you have to kind of control your own suspicions. Don't always be suspicious. One needs to respect other people's language. Don't be so eager to condemn it.

Interviewer: Tell me a little about that new school at Horse Creek. Is it still there?

Mother: No, it's gone. All you see is foundation and the community houses that grew around it. At the time they built the school there were no community houses.

Interviewer: So the students had to walk a long way?

Mother: No, they had a bus. That's the other thing, the U.S. government started having buses and would bring these kids to school. They didn't have to go to boarding school. Before that everybody had to go to boarding school. But now, they are building schools closer to home. Harvey was the bus driver when he was around, but eventually, when we went to Pine Ridge, he became Director of the school transportation.

Interviewer: You went to Europe while you were teaching?

Mother: No, the trip to Europe was in 1939, right after I graduated college. I was surprised when the Dean called me in and said he had a call for me from New York. They wanted me to represent the Native Americans. That was a great honor for me. I was so naive about traveling alone, but he said everything would be furnished for me — that I wouldn't have to worry. So, I accepted. I had just a week to prepare before I left. They even purchased me a couple of suitcases, and an overnight bag with my name stamped on them so I could identify my own luggage. I came home first, then my folks took me to the train depot, then I went by train to New York City. I went to the big central station where a lady from the Young Women's Christian Association (YWCA) met me and we went to the YWCA building. I stayed overnight there and met other people coming in for the trip. We had a meeting and we were all briefed on what to do, what to expect; and then, when it was time, we went on a boat that took us from New York City across the bay to New Jersey where the ocean liner was.

Agnes in Europe

Interviewer: You did this by yourself?

Mother: All by myself.

Interviewer: No escort?

Mother: No escort.

Interviewer: That's hard.

Mother: That was in the summer of 1939, when the Dean told me that the government would help me. I guess the Indian Rights Association had selected me and were paying for all the expenses, but the Federal Government, in addition to that, wanted me to study co-operatives. I told you about going to Copenhagen, Denmark to the People's International College which had a course in co-operatives. How the course was taught was we would have a class and then they would take us out to the different cooperatives to observe whether it was an animal co-operative, or a poultry co-operative, or whatever it was. It was very interesting.

Interviewer: Part of your mission was to learn about cooperatives?

Mother: Yes, the Federal Government said that
               they wanted me to go to that college and
               take those courses.

Interviewer: Did the other members of your group
               attend the co-operative course?

Mother: No.

Interviewer: So you were the only one that went to
               Denmark?

Mother: Yes, because I was the only one repre-
               senting the Bureau of Indian Affairs. I
               don't know what they did. Some of them,
               I think, returned to Paris and did a kind of
               tour, but mine was all business. I had to
               do what the Federal Government wanted.
               I didn't get to Paris, but I did see Berlin. I
               didn't see Adolph Hitler's palace, but I
               saw where his office was.

Interviewer: It's a good thing you didn't see him.

Mother: Yes, he might have cut my nose off. He had his
               men pretty well trained. While I was on that
               train going toward Hamburg, they pillaged
               through my suitcases to see what I had in

there; because, when we got back on the train, it seemed like everything in my suitcase was disturbed. I thought, "Gee, somebody was in here." I think Hitler's men went through my luggage just to see what I had with me.

Interviewer: Before the whole delegation left America, didn't they tell you anything about this threatening situation over there?

Mother: No, not all at.

Interviewer: So you were not prepared for that kind of thing?

Mother: No. Going over we never heard anything. Later, when I began seeing all those Nazi and those officers with swastikas, I began to wonder. I peeked out the train window and I could see airplanes and airports, but what was I going to do? I could only observe what was going on.

Interviewer: Did that scare you?

Mother: Sort of. I thought, "Why are there so many soldiers?" I didn't have any idea there would be a war. I didn't even know why they hated the Jews.

Interviewer: When did you get to know about the Holocaust?

Mother: After we got back, but not until recently did I learn more about the Holocaust. All I know is that I was almost stranded over there.

Interviewer: It's so scary.

Mother: Yes, it was. Then I had to travel back through Copenhagen and Elsinore, that's where the People's International College was; and, then again, I met different groups of people when I made the trip across Sweden. In Copenhagen, we passed by that statue of a girl in the bay.

Interviewer: You mean the mermaid?

Mother: Yes, I thought that was so nice. I wish I'd had a camera, I didn't have a camera. I would buy postcards and try to keep them. But anyway, this little mermaid recently had her head cut off. I don't know why. Why would somebody want to destroy it?

Interviewer: What was your overall impression of Europe.

Mother: I went through it so quickly, but I did try to visit museums. We went to Delft, which is a little village that creates this chinaware. It was a nice place to visit. Europe has a lot of historical places. Harvey was in Europe also. When he went in the Army, they sent him to Europe. After he left, I resigned my teaching job, then I just worked up here at Flandreau Indian School in the garment factory. We made bathrobes, night gowns, and dresses for the boarding schools. I was never good at being a seamstress, but I worked there for a number of years. After Harvey came back from the war, we moved east of Flandreau. That's where we lived for about 5 years. Then Harvey went back to school again under his GI Bill and got his auto mechanics certificate. He worked on automobiles at the Ford garage in Flandreau, and I worked at the garment factory. We lived on a small farm out east of town. The boys went to public school in town. We lived there until 1950, when my father passed away.

BOYS AT FARM

Hepi, Punk, Dick (cousin), and Chaske. (pictured L-R)

Jim Bill

My father had fallen off a horse and got a blood clot that went to his heart. He was still riding horses at his old age. After my dad passed away, I thought I'd go back into teaching again, so I had to go to school and renew my teaching certificate. Harvey was ready now for auto mechanics instead of small engine mechanics. In 1950, we went on relocation to St. Louis, but we weren't very happy. The kids went to school there for one year.

I couldn't ever get a decent job. I had to be a waitress at a little corner cafe and the boys would catch the bus to go to school, all except Jim Bill, he wasn't in school yet. Harvey had to work nights.

Interviewer: Why couldn't you find a job?

Mother: No one wanted an Indian teacher, I guess. I never could find a teaching job. This was another case of discrimination. We were in St. Louis for one year.

It was then that we went to Pine Ridge. Harvey had a sister, Jeanette, living there. Her husband, Tom Conroy, worked in the Bureau of Indian Affairs office and he said, "I think there is a teaching vacancy at the school. They are looking for a teacher right now." I went up there that afternoon and applied. Within the week, we moved in. They gave us a one bedroom apartment on campus and then Harvey got a job at the government garage. The principal of the school wanted someone to head up the transportation of schools, so Harvey transferred to the school garage and managed all the buses. Eventually, they made him supervisor of all the buses on the reservation. So, if the reservation buses had problems, he would go out to the district school or they brought the vehicles to him for repair. There were about six schools on the reservation. It was hectic and the apartment they gave us to live in was a duplex with only one bedroom – the boys had to sleep in the basement. Chuck had sinus problems, because the basement was damp and cold in the winter time; so we sent the boys to a Christian boarding school named Bishop Hare School. Hare School was a home for Indian boys, but they attended public school in Mission, SD.

Interviewer: Was it long away from your home?

Mother: About 100 miles. The boys stayed there, but they came home for holidays.

Interviewer: Were they happy?

Mother: I think they were happy. They had friends there and they were in all the athletics. They played football, basketball, and they were good in track. My boys all graduated from there.

Interviewer: Is it a Catholic school?

Mother: No, Episcopal.

Interviewer: You went to Chadron State College?

Mother: Yes, every other year you have to go back to school to renew your teaching certificate so my principle said, "Agnes, why don't you take courses required for a Masters." I don't remember what year I got my Masters from Chadron State. I think it was 1956.

Interviewer: You have an honorary Doctorate degree from Oglala Lakota College.

Mother: Yes, and this past year (1996) I received another award from the National Indian Education Committee. It was held in Rapid City. I fell down at home and couldn't go to receive my award, but my sons had two of my little great granddaughters, Krystal and Amber, received the award for me, along with a shawl that they had given me. When receiving the award, one of the girls, Krystal, said that someday they will be teachers too.

Interviewer: It gave her an idea about what it takes to be a good teacher.

Mother: Yes, one can learn from example. We have nine granddaughters. Eight of them have their degrees. The youngest girl, Scooby, is a Senior at SDSU in Brookings, SD. She will get her degree in December 1997.

Interviewer: Looks like you started a family tradition.

Mother: Well, I think that when they see the difference an education makes they appreciate it more. I was talking to one of my granddaughters the other night. Just listening to her talk, I thought, "Oh boy, she is really on the road to success."

Interviewer: You were at Pine Ridge for 21 years?

Mother: Yes.

Interviewer: Why were you granted an honorary doctoral degree from Oglala Lakota College?

Mother: I helped start the college. They had a hard time with funding; then they didn't have enough money for teachers. My supervisor allowed me to help. When I went off duty at 3:00 in the afternoon, I would work until 4:00 teaching college courses, and then I would teach evening classes. So I taught elementary all day and taught college courses during the night.

Interviewer: You were teaching at the college level?

Mother: Yes, some of the teachers aides that wanted degrees would ride to class with me. I taught Principles of Education, History of Education, etc.

Interviewer: What do you specialize in teaching?

Mother: I teach history, languages, English Literature, and education. All except math classes. I'm not a math teacher, but Harvey is and my son, Jim Bill, is a math major.

Interviewer: How many of your sons graduated from college?

Allen (Chuck) Ross
B.S., Black Hills State University
M.Ed., Arizona State University
Ed.D., W. Colorado University
A.B.D.*, University of Minnesota

Kenneth (Punk) Ross
B.S., Black Hills State University
M.Ed., N. Arizona University
Ph.D., University of Minnesota

Duane (Hepi) Ross
B.S., Black Hills State University
M.Ed., University of South Dakota

James (Jim Bill) Ross
B.S., Black Hills State University
M.Ed., Arizona State University
A.B.D.,* University of Minnesota

* A.B.D.: All but dissertation.

Mother: All four of them. Jim graduated from college in teaching.

Interviewer: What do you think about the fact that teachers are not well rewarded? When I graduated college, they showed me this salary table. The top salary was computer science -- annual salary about $45,000. Near the bottom, the teacher's annual salary was $18,000. To me it's not right, I

89

mean a teacher is an educator, and an educator is the most important person for the children.

Mother: I feel the same way. I think the teachers are very important.

Interviewer: What I mean is that teachers are not appropriately rewarded. I wanted to become an anthropologist or history teacher in high school; but, when I looked at the salary, I said, "No way." Not enough money number one and that's why I am asking. Why such a huge discrepancy and even disrespect for this very noble occupation. In this country that is not very well accepted. Do you have any idea about this poor treatment.

Mother: I don't think the people realize how important a teacher is until they lose a good teacher. People don't seem to appreciate what those teachers have done until it is too late and they have lost them. A lot of the good teachers don't complain. Like myself, after getting a four year degree, then having them put you through another couple years of internship, and then paying you $45.00 a month for the first year.

Interviewer: That's poor pay.

Mother: That's the way I started out. I would just as soon have stayed at the teaching level. Instead of having people push me up into administration, like my supervisor who said, "Agnes, get your Masters." So I was sort of pushed up to be a teaching supervisor, where I was to teach other teachers. It's so hard to teach adults who are also striving. I would liked to have stayed as a kindergarten teacher.

Interviewer: You don't regret what they have done?

Mother: No, it sort of came naturally. I never really had to apply for a job. I felt as if I wasn't deserving of the promotions they'd give me. A lot of people don't think that way -- they say I'm worth it.

Interviewer: Very few think like you anymore. So, you retired in 1972?

Mother: Yes, after 34 years of teaching. It's great

being retired 25 years, but I have worked just as hard in that 25 years trying to teach little kids, college kids, and helping the Oglala Lakota College. I have helped colleges in the eastern part of the state also.

Interviewer: What is a School Enrollment Committee?

Mother: It's a school committee to control the activity. Bishop Hare school is where my boys went to school, so they asked me to be a parent representative.

Interviewer: Were you part of the Health Board?

Mother: Yes, these boards are for the tribal members. Before we retired and came back to Flandreau in 1972, there was no Indian Health Care here at all. The federal government said we will take care of your health, so I pressured them to set up a clinic here -- now we have this nice clinic. I was on the Health Board for years and also started to set rules and regulations for our CHR (Community Health Representative).

Interviewer: The clinic is to serve the Indian population?

Mother: It is for the Indians, funded by the Federal Government, but it is under the direction of this Health Board. I don't belong to any Boards any longer. I was also on the Tribal Enrollment Committee. We didn't have any secretaries, no one to keep track of the records for this Dakota community, so we set up Enrollment. We worked to find out who the original people were who came here and who their descendants were. We looked at when they were born and where they were born. I sent the Enrollment Records to the Bureau of Indian Affairs.

Interviewer: How did you determine the qualifications to be an Indian.

Mother: They had to be born of Indian parentage. Like in my grandmother's case, she was a full blood Dakota and the father of her child was a white man, which made my father half. Now, if my father had married a white woman, then we would drop my degree of Indian blood down to a quarter degree Indian blood. Every time you inter-marry with a non-Indian, you would lower your Indian blood. If you fall below a quarter degree Indian blood, you are no longer considered an Indian. It took quite a while to get the records finalized. I was on the Enrollment Committee for a long time. We had to do a lot of research.

Interviewer: It was a big responsibility.

Mother: Yes, it is.

Interviewer: Have you ever come across a case like this? This person is full blooded, but was raised among white people as an adopted person. Therefore, he grew up in a white community, which has been done by people like the Mormons. Have you ever come across any cases like that? The person doesn't know who he/she is but, after they grew up, they wanted to be on the Tribal Roles?

Mother: There are a lot of them coming back -- looking for their roots. My cousin's grandson came back just recently. His father died when he was little and his mother couldn't raise him, so he was adopted out by some white people in California. He finally found his way back here to this reservation. His name is Jay Jackson and he is my mother's brother's grandchild. He spent a whole year here and they didn't like the cold weather, so they went back south where it is warm. Anyway, he was satisfied; he finally found his roots. He said, "Now I can tell my grandchildren where my grandfather was buried."

Interviewer: Interesting.

Mother: They have do to a little research to find out for themselves. It's to satisfy your inner self.

Interviewer: The Tribal Rolls can help them search for their identity.

Mother: We have the Tribal directories. A person need only research by phone or by writing to the tribe.

Interviewer: Do you fish?

Mother: Oh, I used to. When we were little, I think

we lived on fish called Bullheads all summer long, because we lived where the river went right by our back door. Mom would fry those Bullheads and my grandmother would take the heads of the Bullhead and boil them for fish soup. She liked the soup.

John/Ida Allen and children
(Left - right) Johnny Allen Jr., John Allen; (three girls - top to bottom) Clara, Dorothy, Margaret; Ida Allen holding (baby) Charlie; Agnes (far right). Photo was taken in 1917.

Nowadays everything is so different. It's something we all should experience. Now, I can go back and reflect.

We used to go up on the hillside and look for turnips. We used to run ahead of Grandma and identify them for her. She would always give thanks, bless the plant, and offered a short prayer thanking God for giving us this food. She would dig it up and, if it had gone to seed, she took the seeds and replanted them in the hole where she had dug up the plant, then she would cover the seeds all up again.

Interviewer: Is it the same as when the boys would go hunting?

Mother: When they'd go hunting plant medicines, we had to go to Minnesota. There is one plant that a lot of our people still use for fighting colds and infections of the lungs. We call it sinkpetawote. Translated it's called muskrats food. They grow in the marshy places up north in Minnesota and Wisconsin. When we go up there, Harvey always takes the grandkids along with him to show them how to harvest them. One time, when a gentleman went with them, they went down and located some sinkpetawote in the marshy places. Harvey took his tobacco out and said a prayer for the plants, and then he had the boys dip it up. This gentleman said, "Now I know why this medicine didn't work for me. I didn't say a prayer - I didn't give thanks." That was the way the Indians did it. He was a modern Indian. A lot of the young people don't know what these things are. It's been forgotten as each generation goes by, but we have a few young people that are still interested.

Not too long ago, four or five years ago, my granddaughter, Kim (who is half Navajo), had a permanent. You know what I mean, curl up your hair. I don't know if they burnt her scalp or what, but she lost a big patch of hair, and she didn't know what to do. At the Sun Dance, Harvey said, "Your people (meaning Navajo) have medicine for that." She said, "We do?" Harvey said, "When you get home, you go out in the desert and you find a Yucca plant, we call it soapweed because the roots are used for soap. When you dig down there's a tubular part and that's what they use to wash their hair." He said Navajo people wash their hair with that. So, when she got home, she went to her old Navajo grandma that lives on the reservation, and she said, "Grandma, that's what Grandpa Ross told me." "That's right," she said, "Go out, get some, and use it." So, she did it and her hair started to grow back. She's got beautiful hair now. Different tribes have different things that are familiar to their area. In the southern states, they have yucca; here, we have soapweeds. I have been trying to grow some and I dug the root up and planted some, but the rabbits ate it up last winter. Now Harvey has another one growing over here and he said he thinks it has taken root now. He had it fenced off, so the rabbits couldn't get to it in the winter time.

Interviewer: They grow in dry country in the south. It is hard to grow them up here in the north.

Mother: It would be unless you had it on a high plain, up where the water would run off.

Interviewer: Tell me about all these canned goods downstairs.

Mother: I think I mentioned a few of them -- the muskrat food, sweet potatoes, some are fruits, some are vegetables, and some are medicines.

Interviewer: Where are the sweet potatoes?

Mother: I don't have any because they are hard to preserve. These are things that we dried in the sun and they last forever. They are not perishable. Because long ago we didn't have refrigeration, we had to dry things in the sun. You know why they call the white people, wasicu? There is a story behind it. Our ancestors would butcher the deer or elk, then they would hang the meat out to dry. The early trappers would sneak up at night and steal our dried meat. When they stole the meat they even took the fat. That's what wasicu means, "take the fat". That's kind of strange, because the white people are so critical of things being fatty, but still they would take the fat too. They fried a lot of their foods then, but the Indians never did fry anything at that time. But look at how thin that meat was and it's dried. They would pound the dried meat and mix it with cherries to make wasna.

Interviewer: It takes a sharp knife to make it that thin.

Mother: That's right. We knew how the meat was layered, so we would cut the meat in layers. We call this to Kabla the meat. The white people called our people Isantee (lived by the knife). But long ago our people didn't have any knives. Our people used the clam shell. They used the sharp edge to cut or to peel or scrape, and then they also used the clam shell for a spoon -- like a ladle. In Dakota, one would say tuki-hasan (tuki - spoon) (hasan - cutter), because the clam shell was used to cut. You put the two words together for spoon-cutter. So, that was our name many, many years ago before the white people came and brought the knives. Tuki hasan, clam shell users or spoon cutter people.

Interviewer: I heard you used buffalo stomach as a pot?

Mother: Yes, they did before my time. The traders brought us metal pots way back in the 1600's. When we used the stomach to cook in, they didn't put it directly over the fire; they would put water in the stomach pot, then add hot rocks to the water and let the water boil.

Interviewer: How did the people prepare meat or vegetables after it was dried?

Mother: You would have to soak it overnight to soften it, or you put it into that boiling water for a long time.

Interviewer: The word I was trying to remember was pemmican.

Mother: I think that is a French word.

Interviewer: Dried buffalo meat?

Mother: We call this wasna. Dried meat and dried cherries mixed together. We Mdewakanton have the corn. Our people had small bins. In the summertime, they would take their corn and cook it on the cob and then scrape it off and dry it in the sun. Dried corn will last forever. When corn is scraped off the cob, this is where the clam shell is used. We used to help our

102

grandma. You take this clam shell and you go down the row of corn. You just cut the kernel off the cob. Later, my grandma used a tablespoon to do the scraping, but she would hold the tablespoon upside down.

As a youngster, we used to go to the river and dig clam shells. Then my father or my grandma would peel them open, and some of them would have pearls in them. I remember one time, when we had a great big pile of shells, my dad sold them to some salesman that came around. They made buttons out of them. So, my dad used to make money off our labor.

Interviewer: Nothing is wasted that way.

Mother: No, nothing is wasted and we helped all the time. No matter what the weather, we hunted for the fruits, vegetables, and roots. As we grew older, my dad acquired cattle and the herd grew. We did the chores in caring for the cattle.

Interviewer: Tell me, just one recipe that used this dried corn.

Mother: It's like rice, you just put it in with your meat, whatever your stew meat might be. It makes wahanpi (soup) and that's our favorite, dried corn soup.

Interviewer: Just by throwing the corn into the boiling water with the meat? Did it soak overnight?

Mother: Well, you can probably help the cooking process, but I never do. Like I do rice — wash them off and throw them in the kettle. We didn't have any wild rice around here, so wild rice was a treat. In Minnesota, we used to gather the wild rice. Nowadays, when people treat us with wild rice, boy that's something. We love wild rice soup.

Interviewer: When you go to a fancy restaurant, they serve wild rice. It is very expensive.

Mother: Yes, I know it is. Some of our people still go to Wisconsin. I worked in Wisconsin for three years and I would watch the Ojibwa Indians as they went out to gather the wild rice.

Interviewer: What does it look like?

Mother: It's a plant that grows out there in the lakes. They would go through the plants with their boats and they'd either tear the tops off or some of the old Indians used to just kind of pound it and the rice would fall into the boat. Have you seen wheat grow? It's like that. Our people used the wild wheat too, like wild rice. After our tribe came here from Minnesota, we didn't have the wild rice, because it doesn't grow here.

Interviewer: Which staple is more common to your people?

Mother: A lot of people preferred the corn, because there was a lot of it and, when our tribe came over here, they had big fields of corn. There is a different type of corn that we call Indian Corn. I don't know what the white people call it, but we make hominy out of it. My grandmother had to use a special kind of a wood; we depend upon the ash tree for a lot of things. It has to be ash wood. She would build a fire with it the night before and in the morning she would take the ashes from the firepit and then she would shake it down, screen it down, so she had only the powder. She'd take the powder and put it with this corn and boil it. It looked like cooking corn in mud to me.

Interviewer: What are the ashes for?

Mother: To get rid of the kernel shell. Nowadays, the white people use lye to make hominy. Well, that is what wood ash contains -- lye. That was the ingredient that helped the outer husk of the corn kernel fall off. Then when the corn was ready for cleaning, we would have to take it to the well, we kids did, and we pumped water and washed it. Then you worked that corn until the heart of the corn, the little tiny black thing, came off.

Interviewer: Hominy is yellow and that is white.

Mother: Sometimes this was blue too, because the Indian corn comes in different colors --

could be red, could be blue. This is phas-dayopi (hominy).

Interviewer: Is the bean also native to this area?

Mother: Yes, we grew beans here too. A story is that the field mice gathered the beans and stored them underground for their winter feed, but the Indians would go and take the mice's nest of beans, but they gave thanks as they did this. In the place of the beans, they would place corn so the mice would have something to eat during the winter. Ominica means beans.

Interviewer: So they grow wild?

Mother: They don't anymore. I don't know where they plant them now,

Interviewer: Can you still find wild turnips?

Mother: They are hard to find around here anymore. I think if you go back to the prairie, Rosebud and Pine Ridge, there you could still find them. I doubt if there is much.

This is a chokecherry. You can pound (grind) this and put it with the meat. This is one of our favorites. The cherry juice and the cherries themselves are sacred to the Dakota. In our ceremonies, we have a healing service and, when the people come for healing, they offer them cherry juice and some wasna.

Interviewer: Do cherries have healing power?

Mother: Yes, nowadays, they say cherries are the best all purpose medicinal fruit.

I go to a lot of public schools to lecture on Dakota culture. There were some young boys who had a question, "Is it true that you worship many spirits?" I said, "We believe like you believe that there is only one God. And we believe also that he has created everything upon this earth for us. If God has created everything upon this earth, all living things like trees and flowers and birds and animals, then within them is the spirit of God; and we should be thankful. We admire them -- we try to protect them." The next morning I had a call from a Catholic priest, he asked me "Will you come tomorrow and speak to the people in my church?" I said I couldn't. But that is how religious our people were. Religion isn't just going to a church and worshipping once a week for us. Every morning when the sun comes up, we should be thankful. When the sun goes down, we give thanks for bringing us safely through the day. So, it is things like that that people should try to understand about what is behind the Indians' way of life.

Interviewer: I think Christianity was the same thing long ago, however they forgot many things.

Mother: Exactly. Some people don't go to church, because they neglect to recognize these old time truths.

Interviewer: What is the secret of such a long marriage? What makes your marriage so successful?

Agnes/Harvey (friends), 1939

Mother: I don't really know. But Harvey's mother was nervous a lot of the time, so he is nervous also. I'm calm. They say you marry your opposite, maybe that's why we are married for so long. Speaking of marriage, we were married December 23, 1939 at Valentine, Nebraska. Harvey was attending school for aeronautical engineering and was home for Christmas vacation. I had my teaching degree from N.A.U., so I was teaching at Horse Creek

School on the Rosebud Reservation. We had known each other for five years. He finished his course and Curtis Wright Factory in Buffalo, New York hired him right away.

I resigned my teaching job in 1941 and we moved to Buffalo. We didn't stay very long, of course, I was pregnant with Kenneth. So Chuck and I came home and Harvey stayed in Buffalo. Harvey worked over there until they closed down. Curtis Wright sold out to McDonnell Aircraft in St. Louis, so that is where he was transferred. We went to St. Louis, but war was declared in December, and every so often he would get this letter from the recruiter and he would have to report his status. I don't know why they kept bothering him -- because they needed soldiers I suppose. In the mean time, he had a first cousin, by the name of Jack Raymond, who was overseas and got killed.

Interviewer: Where did he get killed?

Mother: He was in Africa, then they went to Italy. Anyway he got killed in the landing at Normandy, France. Harvey thought about that and said, "I should be over there." I said, "Well, it is up to you." Harvey felt strongly that he should volunteer to go, so I said OK. I came home when he volunteered for the Army. Hepi was born while he was overseas.

Interviewer: Did Harvey serve in North Africa?

Mother: No, he didn't go to North Africa. He ended up in General Patton's 3rd Army assigned to the 94th infantry. Harvey said he walked all the way across France. He fought in the Battle of the Ardennes.

Interviewer: Please tell me your stories of your childhood.

Mother: Well, I liked being with my grandmother and hunting fruits and vegetables and helping her dry foods. Then later on as, I guess, my dad became more prosperous and owned cattle, we would go milking and eventually had a cream separator. We poured the milk through and it separated the cream from the milk. But before that, we had big crock that mother used to put the milk in and then the cream rises on the top of the milk. She had some kind of a scoop or ladle and just scooped the cream off – separated the cream from the milk. Then we had one more crock with stompers that made the butter. We did all that. Later on, we had the cream separator and that was where you poured the milk on top and it went through this machine and it had two spouts. The milk went one way and because the cream was heavier, it went the other way. My dad and mother used to take the cream to the cream station and sell the cream. We raised chickens and sold the eggs. Now, of course, they do all these things in great big poultry farms. I don't think individual families do much of this anymore, but that's the way we were raised.

Interviewer: So you are living in two worlds?

Mother: Well, I have learned to live in the modern world. I do things differently now. I go to the store to buy it rather than make things.

Interviewer: So, these are things you were doing before you started attending elementary school, but of course you resumed that while attending school. Do you remember anything, any memorable thing that happened during your elementary school years? Did you walk a long way to your school?

Wagon used to travel to school.

Mother: We walked to school. But in the winter time, my dad would hitch up a horse and wagon. We kids would climb in and he would take us to school if the snow was too deep or extra cold. There was a farm house halfway to school and a sweet, German lady would see us coming; she'd meet us at the gate to see that we were wrapped up, so that we didn't catch cold. When she thought we were too cold, she would take us in the house and warm us up before we went on again. She was awfully nice to us.

Interviewer: School started in September and you went until December for winter break?

Mother: No, we didn't have a winter break. We had Christmas off, but there was no such thing as Christmas break. In college, they had a two week break or something like that; but, in public school, they didn't do that.

Interviewer: You attended school until May, then there's a summer break, three months. So you resumed in September again. During summer break, what did you do?

Mother: We just stayed home and helped with the gathering of fruits and vegetables. I remember in early spring, when the sap began to come up in the trees, we had maple trees down along the river and my dad would take a tree auger and drill out a hole in the tree. He would put a little wooden spigot in the hole and put a pail underneath, a gallon syrup pail, and the sap would drip into that pail. Later, we would pick up the maple syrup pail and my grandma or my mom would boil it. That's how they made the maple syrup. If she wanted sugar, she would continue boiling the syrup, then take these muffin tins and fill them up with this juice and set them out – then that would harden. Isn't that something, how they would do it. They would pound the dried maple syrup and make sugar or you could just leave it as syrup.

Interviewer: It must have been a fun job making maple syrup.

Mother: Yes. I liked maple syrup on pancakes in the morning. You very seldom bought a loaf of bread. Mother baked bread. When Dad went to town to purchase something, he would buy a big sack of flour.

Interviewer: Did you bake bread yourself?

Mother: Once in awhile, but every now and then I make some fry bread. It is made with flour, biscuit dough-like, and you fry it.

Interviewer: Are there any stories you can tell me about wild animals?

Mother: I remember my dad going out to trap. He always trapped in the wintertime. He would trap for beavers or muskrat; he had a gun, so he would bring home rabbits to eat. But the beaver and muskrat were for the purpose of making money, not for family consumption. He would skin the hides out and dry them, then sell the hides.

Interviewer: Would he trap in this area?

Mother: Yes, they would go where the lakes are and trap the surrounding rivers and creeks.

Interviewer: Would the people hunt skunk?

Mother: Yes, for their pelts. They sold the pelts and the Indian people used the skunk oil for medicine.

Interviewer: How did they get skunk oil?

Mother: From the fat, they rendered the fat. I remember drinking it for a sore throat.

Interviewer: How did they kill bad odor?

Mother: I guess you just got used to it. Especially

when you had a chest cold, they would rub you down with it and then they would put a diaper or something over it. You could inhale the fumes, like breathing Vicks or Mentholatum, or similar to that. The vapors I suppose cleared your sinuses.

Interviewer: You said your older sister didn't like school much.

Mother: I started school when I was five. I had to be her companion.

Interviewer: Is there any memorable instance or event during elementary school?

Mother: No, all of them were good to me, maybe I was good to them. I don't know. But some of my favorite teachers were elementary teachers. They complain now of not getting any help. A lot of the teachers are very helpful, especially to minorities who couldn't speak the language fluently. My sister and I didn't know any words in English before we started school, so I would see that she came to school. I was very active. I was curious about things and wanted to learn. I often sit down now and wonder how things came to be or how things work. Out of nine children, I am the only one that got a college degree. My other sisters went to Haskell and took typing, but I didn't want to be a typist. I wanted to work with children. So, when I first went into the U.S. Government Service, I was sort of a recreation aide, I think that is what they call it now. A recreation aide is a person who would help after class hours with the girls, and work with them in sports or some athletic activity.

Interviewer: So that kept you busy during the entire day?

Mother: Yes, that was my job during the school year. I would teach kids after school until they went to bed. My job was over until the next morning, then you would help them get ready for school again. I did that for a couple years. I had this one teacher friend, she was a regular classroom teacher, she encouraged me to go to summer school with her because she had her degree.

Interviewer: Later on, you were Program Chairman for the college YWCA. What does a Program Chairman do?

Mother:	Organizes monthly meetings, finds speakers or songs to sing, or plans what you want to do. I thought and planned.
	This is one of my teachers. Her name was Ellen too. She always wanted to get me to sing in the church choir. I did sing with the chorus and we sang from the Grand Canyon in Arizona on Easter morning. We had to go up there the night before and be there at Easter sunrise to sing.
Interviewer:	So you took a long trip up there?
Mother:	No, I was at Northern Arizona University, so it wasn't to far from Flagstaff. I liked the choir director. He was a graduate of Yankton College here in South Dakota.
Interviewer:	Was he part Indian?
Mother:	No, I don't think he was part Indian. We went up there on horses, stayed overnight in the canyon, and almost froze to death. It was very cold. I don't know who's idea it was. They had a little alter set there. I don't know if they still do that or not. The choir was broadcast over the radio.

Interviewer: During 1936 to 1938, is that when you attended Northern Arizona University?

Mother: Yes, I went there in 1936 and graduated in 1938.

Interviewer: Did you receive a bachelor's degree?

Mother: Yes, that is where I got my bachelor's degree. There were a couple of Indian boys that went to school there. There was one boy, I think he was a boxer, another friend later became the Governor of Arizona. Another one of my classmates became the Director of Education for the State of California. Occasionally, you come across some of your friends and learn how their careers have gone.

I was business manager of the Women's Athletic Association and the Young Women's Christian Association Program Chairman at Northern Arizona University.

Interviewer: Is the Northern Arizona University still there?

Mother: Yes, and not too long ago it was one of the top ten outstanding teacher education colleges nationwide. It produced some good, sympathetic teachers. You have to be interested in your students for the students to progress. That is very important to students. That's why, as I progressed up the ladder, I never did apply for a higher position. I was always selected and, more or less, forced to do that. I would have just as soon stayed with my kindergarten children.

When I first started out in education, since I was bilingual, they gave me all the little kindergarten kids who couldn't speak English. I had to work with them to get them ready for first grade.

Oglala Community School - First Grade, 1958

Interviewer: Were you one of the first American Indian teachers who taught school?

Mother: I don't know. I do know I was the first American Indian Teacher of the Year in the State of South Dakota. When I was selected as the Teacher of the Year, it came about through the Bureau of Indian Affairs when Ben Rifle, a Lakota man, was B.I.A. Area Director. He presented me the certificate. In his speech, he stated I was born to be a teacher. Later, Mr. Rifle became a U.S. Congressman.

Agnes Ross - 1958
"Teacher of the Year"

Interviewer: You launched your teaching career in 1938 at Pine Ridge for $45.00 monthly.

Mother: During my first year teaching, I received $45.00 a month to be a teacher. Nowadays, we hear complaints, teachers say, "I'm worth more."

Interviewer: You have many artifacts to hand down to your children and grandchildren.

Mother: That's what our youngest grandson, David, said. "Someday I am going to build a big building, it will be a museum, and I am going to put all of Grandpa's things in it." Grandpa has a lot of things down there in what he calls his cultural room. Not only his paintings, but all his plant medicine and cultural things. We met a person at the Sun Dance and she works with an Indian tribe on a Canadian Reserve. She said, "Harvey, your things should be in a museum."

Interviewer: When is the Sun Dance?

Mother: It's the 29th of July in the Black Hills. We call the first day "Tree Day", then they will dance for four days and will end on August 2nd. It is just a few miles from Cheyenne Crossing.

Harvey: The Tree Day is the 29th of July. That's when they take the old tree down and they put the new one in. That's the start of the ceremony. The dancers go out and cut another tree and bring it in; they never let it touch the ground. Before the tree is erected, you tie prayer flags to the tree. The tree is very sacred.

Interviewer: What kind of tree?

Mother: Cottonwood. Up there, there are no cottonwoods; they use aspen. It's related to the cottonwood.

Harvey: When you come to the Sun Dance, bring food to eat. There is nothing out there.

Interviewer: No supermarket, no restaurant?

Harvey: No nothing.

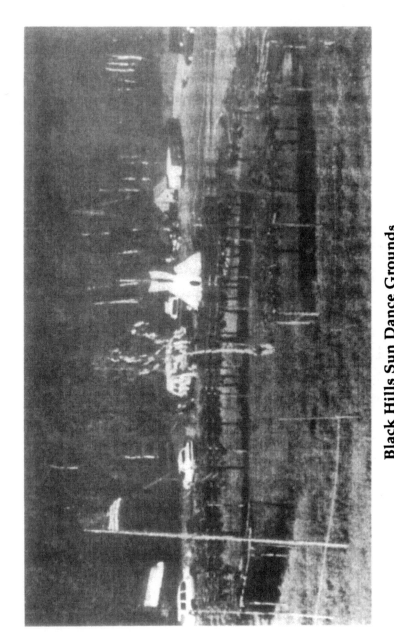

Black Hills Sun Dance Grounds
Flandreau Santee Sioux Tribal Land

126

Mother: But you are supposed to fast; that's what we do.

Interviewer: Even if I don't dance, I still have to fast?

Mother: Even if you don't dance. You honor them by fasting with them. Because they dance for you.

Interviewer: They don't eat at all, even after sunset?

Mother: No, the dancers don't eat at all. Some have liquids. It's an individual pledge whether they drink or not -- but no food.

Harvey: When you come, come prepared to look, listen, and learn -- ask questions.

Interviewer: What Dr. Ross said in his book that experience is the best teacher -- you have to feel it and figure it out by yourself, so let's not ask so many questions. That seems to be what he is saying.

Harvey: But, if you don't understand, you should ask questions.

Interviewer: I might ask some questions, but on the other hand, because I come from a background that many things I am able to figure out that comes from my own cultural background. There are so many similarities. I feel more comfortable just listening, maybe occasional questions.

Interviewer: When I asked you about the spiritual thing yesterday, Harvey gave me the impression that women are not supposed to talk about these things.

Mother: There are a lot of things that women don't participate in -- the men have some ceremonies for men only. You don't know what they talk about or what they do. The women sweat separately. Women have to sweat in their own way.

I've been going to Sun Dance for over 20 years, because that's how long my sons have been dancing. I've seen other Sun Dances and it seems like they have too many dancers. For me, it causes too much confusion. At the Black Hills Sun

Dance, it's a small group and people can concentrate on their prayers. When the sun goes down, everybody goes to sleep for the night. At the larger Sun Dances, I've noticed that people stay up late. Dancing all day, the dancers want to rest at night, because the dancers get up before the sun comes up. The dancers hold a sweat lodge before they go in the circle -- it takes a lot of energy.

Interviewer: It must be painful to pierce?

Mother: I don't know. They don't seem to mind.

Interviewer: The dancers dance until the skin breaks?

Mother: Yes, until the skin breaks.

Interviewer: So, do you know of any medicine woman personally?

Mother: No, I don't know of any today. My Great Grandmother Standing Cloud was a medicine woman. My mother had a medicine bundle which was given to her by her Grandmother Standing Cloud. My mother whose Indian name is

Wanakaza win (Old Lady Behavior Woman) never used the bundle because she was raised a Christian, but my mother had a lot of respect for this bundle. Where some people might have just discarded it, she kept it in reverence, and passed it on to me. I took this bundle to Dawson No Horse and asked him what I should do with it. Dawson said it was a female medicine bundle, and that I should pass it on to a female member of the family. "The person in possession of such a bundle should pass it on," he said, "when they have a dream to do so."

(Hupahu Sna Sna Win)   (Habya Mani)
Mary Standing Cloud   **Gus Standing Cloud**
103 years old   Mary's husband
photo taken in 1930

Tiyospaye Matriarchy

Ida Wakeman (Agnes Allen's mother), was orphaned shortly after her birth. Ida Wakeman's mother, Judith MniTanka, had no brothers or sisters. Normally, in a situation like this, Judith's sister would raise her children, since in the Traditional Dakota society a mother's sister is also considered the mother. Hence, children of

---

* Tiyospaye means extended family.

131

sisters are brothers and sisters — there is no concept of cousins. So now the duty of raising Judith's children became the responsibility of her mother Winona. But, Winona had fled to Canada to escape the soldiers who were hunting the Santee after the eight week war of 1862. Two years later, she died of exposure trying to return to her family, who were now relocated by the U.S. Government to Fort Thompson, South Dakota. So Winona's sister Mary (Martha) Standing Cloud (Hupahu Sna Sna Win) welcomed the Matriarchy Duty of raising Ida and her siblings.

Ida, at an early age, learned to talk like a Grandma and act like a Grandma. Hence, she was given the name Wanakaza Win (Old Lady Behavior Woman). It was this same Grandmother Mary (Martha) that helped raise Agnes. Agnes was 20 years old when Mary (Hupahu Sna Sna Win) passed away in 1930. The Tiyospaye Matriarchy was then passed on to Ida Wakeman. After raising nine children of her own, one Grandchild, and two Hunka children, Ida passed away in 1980. Agnes, being the only living daughter of Ida, became the New Matriarch. Wihopa (Agnes) is now the oldest living member of the Flandreau Santee Sioux Tribe and, as the keeper of a female medicine bundle, Wihopa is also the Sun Dance Grandmother for the Black Hills Sun Dance.

TIYOSPAYE MATRIARCHY

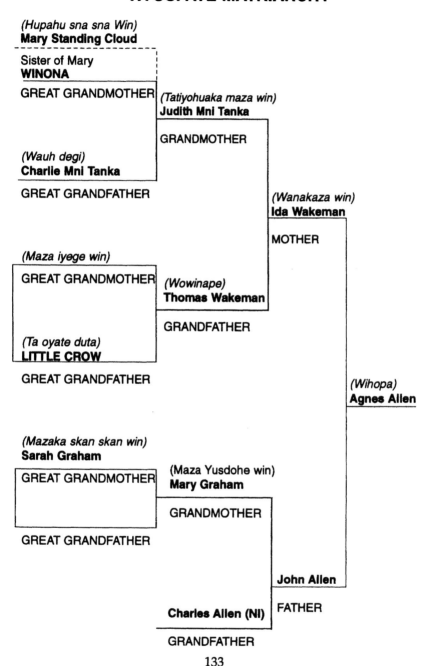

(Hupahu sna sna Win)
Mary Standing Cloud

Sister of Mary
WINONA

GREAT GRANDMOTHER

(Tatiyohuaka maza win)
Judith Mni Tanka

GRANDMOTHER

(Wauh degi)
Charlie Mni Tanka

GREAT GRANDFATHER

(Wanakaza win)
Ida Wakeman

MOTHER

(Maza iyege win)

GREAT GRANDMOTHER

(Wowinape)
Thomas Wakeman

GRANDFATHER

(Ta oyate duta)
LITTLE CROW

GREAT GRANDFATHER

(Wihopa)
Agnes Allen

(Mazaka skan skan win)
Sarah Graham

GREAT GRANDMOTHER

(Maza Yusdohe win)
Mary Graham

GRANDMOTHER

GREAT GRANDFATHER

John Allen

FATHER

Charles Allen (NI)

GRANDFATHER

133

Interviewer: What are the herbs or medicines she used with the bundle?

Mother: The bundle was not used in that way, but they say she was good at treating people. I know my mother used some things that Grandma still treated us with. The bundle was used for female power.

Interviewer: You didn't learn these things at college.

Mother: No, I certainly didn't.

Interviewer: You think nowadays when an Indian student goes to college that there should be some course for youngsters to keep the tradition going?

Mother: We had a governor named Mickelson, that said, "Why don't they teach Lakota?" Now, as a result, they teach Lakota in the schools.

Interviewer: Do you attend traditional ceremonies quite often?

Mother: Once a year -- the Sun Dance. I used to help out with the sweats. If somebody is sick, everyone wants to pray for that person. They would get together with prayers in a sweat lodge. We have a sweat lodge down here and our sons use it every now and then. I used to participate in the sweat lodge but, in the past two years, I haven't gone into the sweat lodge.

Interviewer: Tell me about Flandreau Indian School where you have attended. At that time when you were attending this school, was it just for some kids around this area or nationwide?

Mother: Originally, the school was to be built for our community. I don't know when other tribes started coming in. Later, the qualifications were either to be orphaned or if they lived too far from a school. The school used to have about 800 students, but now they have a lot less.

Interviewer: Is it because the Indian students are starting to attend public schools?

Mother: Well, they probably are, but I think the students are close to a school now, so they don't have to come here.

Interviewer: Is the curriculum specific for Indian people?

Mother: No, they have to abide by the public school curriculum. But there was a time, like when I went to school in those early years, that it was more or less a vocational school.

Interviewer: Has learning all these things you have done throughout your life created inside of you some confusion about your identity, about being Indian.

Mother: No, I came back here to my home town and I am proud to have achieved as much as I have being Indian. I think the white people have recognized it and they are very respectful of me.

Interviewer: Is it correct to say that Indian teachers were more help to the students than white teachers?

Mother: Yes, they were. I was on the National Advisory Committee for Teacher Corp. I attended one meeting for the National Teacher Corp — in Washington, DC. We had representatives from all areas and there were quite a lot of minorities. I think I was the only Indian on the committee who represented the Indian programs. They were asking me to make suggestions on how to improve the curriculum. Imagine, me, working on such committees. I told them the same as I've been telling you.

Interviewer: Your devotion and dedication is so great, that they couldn't find anyone else.

Mother: Maybe that is it.

Interviewer: During that time, there was a big thing going on the Pine Ridge Indian Reservation, the Wounded Knee takeover in 1973 by the American Indian Movement. Can you tell me anything about that?

Mother: No, because we retired and left Pine Ridge in 1972 and this all happened in 1973. I do know that, shortly before that, Robert Kennedy came to the reservation and spoke to the student body. Then he made a trip out to Wounded Knee, to the

137

monument. He took flowers out there and put them on the mass grave. They said that he cried. He mourned for what his people had done. All the bodies were just dumped in this one mass grave -- there is a monument out there. Now, they are talking about making it a National Monument, but the Oglala Tribe themselves would like to control it.

Interviewer: Your career is devoted to Indian education. What are the changes you have observed through all these long years?

Mother: Of course, 70 years ago, my people were still Lakota/Dakota speaking only. Nowadays, I don't think they are confronted with the problem of trying to teach English as a second language. But in my day they were, and that was where I became very handy to the students. I would take the youngsters, even as old as twelve years old, and help them if they couldn't speak the English language. I don't know how to compare it now, because we didn't even have a bilingual program then. Today the high schools and colleges are now trying to reintroduce the Lakota language in the curriculum.

Interviewer: Today's students have more interest and the motivation to learn about their culture.

Mother: All nine of my granddaughters will have their college degrees this year. I am very proud of them. You love your kids and you help them no matter how difficult it is to do. You have to be a good example. But when you get after them, you shouldn't slap them around and kick them out of the house. Those children are your children for life. You don't give up control of them just because they turn eighteen and kick them out of the house. That's what some white people do. Traditionally, that's not the way the Indian people treat their children. You talk softly to them. You try to help them correct mistakes or make a change for the better.

Interviewer: What is the Indian way to be independent. Some children, even if they are 18 or 20, still don't want to be on their own. They want to be dependent on someone else.

Mother: They are that way because that is the old traditional way. In our way, the give away system is used to help those who cannot help themselves. It is more honorable to give than receive was the motto.

Interviewer: Tell me about Indian running, you said you were a very good runner.

Mother: In the beginning, Indians were always afoot. They didn't have any other means of getting places. There were no cars, they didn't even have horses in the early days. When they went hunting, they had to go out on foot; if they were chasing an animal or something, they would have to run after it. After a while, it came naturally for them to be good runners.

Interviewer: Tell me about your marriage, how did you meet Harvey?

Mother: I knew Harvey when I first went to Rosebud Reservation. I had been there two years and Harvey had worked around the school. He wanted to do everything to help. If there was something to carry or something like that, he was very helpful; he was a good friend and a helpful friend.

Then I went away to finish my college. That summer I went to summer school and I was gone for two, going on three years, and then we just bumped into each other again. In the meantime, he had written a couple of times. We renewed our friendship; we always got along and he was always helpful. To this day, if I'm not able to do it, he will mop the floors for me, clean the house, make the bed, and do the laundry; he'll do anything that he sees I can't do. But he says, "The only thing I won't do is cook."

But that's the way it was. We always did things together, I never went anywhere without notifying him, it's friendship with the ability to communicate. It's being able to tell each other what's going on. I think that communication is very important. *

Interviewer: Do you consider that being the secret of your long marriage?

Mother: Yes, that's part of it. As a result, Harvey and I have been married 59 years in December.

Agnes and Harvey Ross
57th Wedding Anniversary

* *The secret to a lasting marriage is an intimate friendship between husband and wife. In a survey, most respondents credit a positive attitude toward their spouse as the reason for a long marriage. Source: Dept. of Human Behavior, San Diego International University.*

Interviewer: When I visited the cemetery up there, I recognized so many Allen's. Are they all related to you?

Mother: We were talking about enrollment yesterday. When the government came in here to enroll people, they didn't want to stop and translate all the names into English like they did on the Pine Ridge and Rosebud reservations, where they have names like Eagle Elk or Red Cloud or Blue Thunder. The government told the Indian people to take an English name, someone that they knew or somebody they had heard about. So most of our people took names that they wanted to take. The other Allen family -- their great grandmother and my grand- mother were friends. When they went to enroll, their grandmother didn't know what name to use. She said to my grandma, "I don't know what name to give my grandchild." Their little boy and my dad were about the same age, they were playmates, so my grandmother said, "Well, take John's name." John Allen, my dad, was born illegitimate by an Army officer named Charles Allen. That's why

143

he had the name Allen. So they took the name of Allen also. That's how the other Allen family got started. It was just a name that they adopted.

Interviewer: That's what happened when the black people were freed. They didn't have any name at all, so they just took their former master's name.

Mother: A lot of Dakota people have hung on to their original names. If we had taken one of my grandmothers' names, our name would be Mni Tanka (Big Water) or my great grandmother's name Mahpeya Najin (Standing Cloud)

Interviewer: Do you have an Indian name?

Mother: I have an Indian name, in fact I have three Indian names. My baby name was Ite Blaksa (Flat Face), because I was so fat; they said I didn't have a nose. Then I had a great uncle, Rev. Sam Hopkins, that came back from Pine Ridge, he was a missionary at Allen, SD. He said, "What an awful name. She's a beautiful girl; you shouldn't name her that." So he named

144

me Wihopa (Pretty Woman). When I moved to Pine Ridge, the old chief Red Cloud used to walk by our house almost every day on his way to town. One day he stopped to visit. He only spoke Lakota. He shook hands with me and he said do you have an Indian name? I said, "Yes, I have an Indian name, Wihopa." "Oh, what a beautiful name," he said, "that must be a Dakota word." He said, "Your name means Beautiful Woman."

Interviewer: Was that the original Red Cloud?

Mother: No, his son. The original Red Cloud was long gone. Anyway, that's what he called me, the second name. About twenty years ago, after a celebration, a medicine man, Dawson No Horse, wanted to introduce me by my Indian name. "She's got a beautiful name," he said, "Wicahpi Iyega Win (Sparkling Star Woman)." I guess he couldn't remember my name, so he called me Sparkling Star Woman.

FAMILY TREE

Ida Wakeman
1890 - 1980

John Allen
1875 - 1950

Clara Allen, 1909 - 1968
Ross Wade

Ross Wade
Don Wade
Jon Wade
Dorothy Wade
Dean Wade

Agnes Allen, 1910 -
Harvey Ross

Allen (Chuck) Ross
Kenneth (Punk) Ross
Duane (Hepi) Ross
James (Jim Bill) Ross

Dorothy Allen, 1912 - 1948
Lawrence Posey

Larry Posey

John Allen, Jr., 1913 - 1954
Codella Johnson

Pauline Allen
John Allen, Jr.
Paulette Allen
Patricia Allen
Cheryl Allen
LeRoy Allen
Debra Allen

Margaret Allen, 1915 - 1946
Cecil Green

No children

Charles Allen, 1917 - 1962

No children

Kenneth Allen, 1919 - 1995
Margaret Crawford

Dick Allen

Vern Allen, 1925 - 1982
Thelma Johnson

Sandra Allen
Dale Allen
Donald Allen
Pamela Allen
Cindy Allen

Donald Allen, 1927 - 1956
Lilo Platner

Shirley Allen

Harvey Ross
(Isnala Najin)

Agnes Allen
(Wihopa)

Allen (Chuck)Ross
(Ehanamani)
Dorothy Brave Eagle

Dana
Dawn

Patsy Denet

Cindy
Sandy
Hok
Fred

Kenneth (Punk) Ross
(Ta Wasu Ota)
Lucille Martin

Kim
Kelly

Duane (Hepi) Ross
(Mni Tanka)
Janet Claymore

Olivia
Nicolas

Sharon Cuny

Duane Jr.
Gregory
Jennifer
Patrick
Margaret
William

James (Jim Bill) Ross
(Ho Wasté)
Viola Miles

Elaine
Richard
David

GREAT GRANDCHILDREN
OF
HARVEY AND AGNES ROSS

Parent

Ryan Ross	)
Larissa Ross	) --------------- Duane Ross Jr.
Jonathan Ross	)
Chandler Ross	) --------------- Greg Ross
Marvin Ross	)
Stephen Ross	) --------------- Patrick Ross
Britteny Ross	) Julie He Crow
Shelby Ross	)
Amber Sierra	)
Montana Sierra	) --------------- Jennifer Sierra
Colton Sierra	) Smiley Sierra
Sharon Ross	) --------------- Margaret Ross
Kirkland Ross	) --------------- Bill Ross
Stephan Ross	) Brandy Big Crow
Krystal Brave Eagle	)
Kelsea Brave Eagle	) --------------- Dana Brave Eagle
Kaitlyn Brave Eagle	)
Santee Ross	) --------------- Sandy Castro
Natalie Castro	)
John Allen	
Theodore Ross	) --------------- Hok Ross
Tatania Ashley	) Verine White Rock
Tyson Ross	) --------------- Fred Ross
	Susan Thompson

HUNKA CHILDREN
OF
AGNES ROSS

Linda Mitchell

Rockee McHugh

Chaude Two Elk

Joan Bird

Jody Luger

Chuck Lewis

"Utilizing the Hunka (adoption) ceremony to increase your Tiyospaye (extended family) is the key to survival. "

Dawson No Horse

SACRED ABOVE IS SACRED BELOW,
taken from Mitakuye Oyasin by A.C. Ross

My brother Hepi told me about an experience he'd had with Dawson No Horse. They were preparing to go into the sweat lodge when Dawson went to the fire pit and picked up a red-hot rock. He turned and brought it to a twelve-year-old boy who stood there also preparing to go into the lodge. The boy took the rock, looked at it, then looked at Dawson. It didn't burn him. Dawson took the rock back and went into the sweat lodge and prayed with it. When he came out of the lodge, he told the boy the reason he could pick up that red-hot rock without being burned was that one day he would be wicasa wakan (holy man). But he said, "This ability will come to you only when you are older, not when you're fifty or sixty -- but when you are an old man."

I began thinking about this incident. There's a common denominator here, I reasoned. I pondered over the question for almost two years. Then I accidently came upon the common denominator. Both

Dawson and the boy were born in the same month. They were both born in March.

Boys Dance Class Graduation, Denver, CO - 1977
(L-R) Harvey Ross and Dawson No Horse

The revelation brought to recall the Cayce readings where Cayce talked about a study called astrology. The word astrology comes from the Latin and Greek and means star speech. According to Cayce, in between earthly lives your spirit visits certain star systems, acquiring the vibration of that star system. When it comes into the next body, it carries the vibration of that star system. The month in which you are born identifies the star system your spirit visited. Being a student of traditional Native American religious thought, I could accept what Cayce said about star systems having vibration. In the traditional D/Lakota philosophy, it is said that everything is alive. The earth is alive, the sun is alive, and the stars are alive.

As I studied this phenomenon, I remember reading about how modern scientists say that everything has a vibration. Everything contains atoms, and it is these atoms that provide the vibration of the object. For instance, scientists say that rocks vibrate, but they're vibrating so slowly that they appear as solids. When you speed up the vibrations, the rock turns into a liquid. Speeding up the liquid vibrations eventually changes the liquid into a gas. The molecules are just vibrating at a different frequency. Traditional D/Lakota holy people say that the rocks are alive -- that they contain a spirit. I wondered if the rock spirit and the rock molecules were the same.

Another example of the ability of rocks to contain vibration is found in the first radio. It wasn't run by electricity, nor was it run by battery. It was operated by the vibrations put out by a rock. This radio was called the crystal radio. I became so intrigued with this idea that I even went out and bought a crystal radio kit. After a few minutes effort, I had it operating. I was simply amazed at how a radio could be run by a rock!

Scientific discoveries that rocks contained vibrations just reinforced my belief that the stars are alive and the possibility of one's spirit acquiring vibrations from them even more believable.

It was at this point in my life that I wanted to acquire more knowledge on astrology. In visiting with my cousin, Elgie Raymond, and his wife, Margaret, I learned that she was a novice astrologer. I asked her, "Where could I get hold of an astrologer who could teach me more about astrology?" She gave me the name of a New Age bookstore in Minneapolis. I called and asked if they knew of an astrologer who could teach me more about star systems, and they gave me the name of Joe Osowski. I phoned Mr. Osowski and found out that he conducted astrology classes. I made an appointment and flew to Minneapolis, proceeding to take some lessons from him.

Joe stated that there are many different kinds of astrology. I said, Which one is the most common in the United States? That's the one I want to learn about. He introduced me to western astrology, which has a geocentric approach. After some explanations and discussions, I bought some books, went home, and started learning more about astrology. It took me a week to construct a birth chart; and, at the end of that time, I wasn't sure that it was right. I called Joe, and he explained things to me over the phone. From that moment on, he became my continuing astrology teacher.

The first activity in constructing a chart is to identify which signs of the zodiac the planets are in and where they are from the horizon. The zodiac is a belt of star constellations that appear around the planet; the planets orbit around the sun. There are twelve constellations that make up the zodiac. The stars of the constellations are positioned in such a way that they are seen to form symbolic objects. They are: Two Fish, a Ram, a Bull, the Twins, a Crab, a Lion, a Virgin, a set of Scales, a Scorpion, an Archer, a Goat, and a Water Carrier. Cayce said that each of these star systems has their own vibrations, each different from the other. Three of these symbols are associated with characteristics spoken of in terms of spiritual vibrations. The three are the Two Fish, commonly called Pisces; the Crab, known as Cancer; and the Scorpion, called Scorpio.

In astrology, it is calculated that if you were born from February 19th to March 22nd, you are known as having the sun in the sign Pisces, or as a Pisces. If your birthdate is between June 24th and July 24th, you are known as Sun in Cancer. If you are born from October 24th to November 22nd, you are called a Scorpio or Sun in Scorpio.

Cayce said the psychic readings that if you were born during any one of those three times, one of the characteristics that will dominate in this life is spirituality. This gave me an idea. I decided to survey the Sun Dancers I knew to find out their birthdates. As I questioned them, I overhead one of them say behind my back, "What is Chuck Ross up to now?" The results of my survey showed that the majority of the Sun Dancers I talked to were born during one of the three times that Cayce outlined as containing spirituality. Since the D/Lakota religion does not proselytize for Sun Dancers, I wondered, "Was it being born with this spiritualism that led these dancers to participate?"

In reading The Portable Jung, edited by Joseph Campbell, I found that even though Jung believed in synchronistic events, he had some reservations about astrology. He decided, therefore, to undertake a thorough investigation of astrology. As a result of his experiments, he was forced to recognize it. After reading this about Jung, I decided I, too, would continue my studies in astrology.

I found that once your spirit has been influenced by the stars and the closer it gets to the earth's plane, it is next influenced by the planets. Just like the stars, the planets have vibration. Each planet vibrates at a distinct frequency. These frequencies then influence your spirit with dominant modes of thought. Nine planets and earth's moon are the major considerations in astrology. These are the planets listed in seriation from the sun outward: Mercury, Venus, Earth, Mars, Jupiter, Saturn, Uranus, Neptune, Pluto. These planets are not in a straight line. The first four are called the inner planets, and they move very fast in their orbits. It takes only a matter of months for them to revolve around the sun.

The remaining five planets, the outer planets, take years to revolve around the sun. When your spirit approaches Earth's plane at birth time, all of the planets are in different positions around the sun. Their position determines how the frequency influences your spirit. They appear in the different signs of the zodiac which have as their background the different constellations. The relationships between the planets are called aspects, which link planet energies together.

The stars, the planets, and Earth's moon are placed in certain positions on a birth chart, a map in the shape of a wheel with twelve spokes. The earth is at the hub, and the signs of the zodiac are on the circumference of the wheel at the points where the spokes touch the rim. Each zodiac sign occupies thirty degrees. While the constellations in the background vary in size, the overlap of the two changing over time is called the precession of the equinoxes. The sign Aries slowly proceeds from Pisces to Aquarius as we progress to the age of Aquarius. The areas between the spokes are called houses.

If two planets are 60 degrees or 120 degrees apart, an easy aspect is formed. This means that the influence from these two planets would be easy for us in this life. Planets 60 degrees apart are called sextile, and those 120 degrees apart are known as a trine, and both sextile and trine indicate easy aspects. If there are three planets, each 120 degrees apart, this formation is called a Grand Trine. The influences from the combined three planets would be easy for a person in this life. If two planets are close together (within eight degrees), this is termed a conjunction, and the influence from these planets have a combined effect on your spirit. Two planets that are 45 degrees, 90 degrees, or 180 degrees apart are called difficult aspects. Influences between planets in these positions would have a more difficult effect on a person's life.

In order to plot a birth chart or star map, there are five things a person needs to know: the latitude and longitude of his birthplace; the day, month, year, and time -- down to the exact minute -- of one's birthdate. With this information, one needs to consult an ephemeris, a book which contains tables giving computed positions of the stars, the planets, and Earth's moon. This information, when plotted, determines which constellations and planets are important in one's life. Some people say, "What star system were you born under?" or "What's your sign?"

Looking through the ephemeris, I wondered, "How long did it take man to develop this book of charts?" As I mused about how old astrology was, I recalled seeing the movie *Marco Polo* , that when Polo went to China in the 1270s, he discovered that the

Chinese were using astrology -- in fact, had been using it for thousands of years. When he returned to Europe and informed the people about what he saw and heard, they told him he was crazy.

As I continued my research in astrology, I learned that once I had plotted a chart and determined the planetary positions and aspects, then I needed to review a book of interpretations. What one first looks for when interpreting a chart is the ascending sign, which is the star system on the eastern horizon at the time of the birth one is looking at. Whatever was coming into ascendance at the time of birth, according to the Cayce readings, was very important.

Reflecting back on the spirituality aspects within charts, I asked Joe Osowski if he would calculate, by computer, some charts on holy people who were born during the three times of the year that were interpreted by Cayce as possessing spiritualism. In addition to spiritual times of the year, Cayce also said that certain planets had specific spiritual qualities: the Moon in a chart is interpreted as an individual having a natural ability to communicate with the unconscious mind; Uranus – that the individual would have psychic powers; Neptune – that the person is seen as being a mystic; and Pluto – that the individual would possess a higher consciousness.

The first chart I asked Joe to do was Dawson No Horse. When I received it in the mail, the initial thing I

STAR MAP

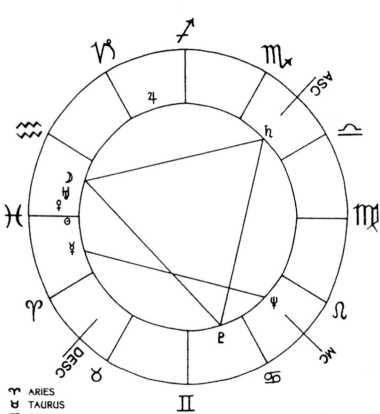

♈	ARIES	
♉	TAURUS	
♊	GEMINI	
♋	CANCER	
♌	LEO	
♍	VIRGO	
♎	LIBRA	
♏	SCORPIO	
♐	SAGITTARIUS	
♑	CAPRICORN	
♒	AQUARIUS	
♓	PISCES	

☽	MOON
☉	SUN
☿	MERCURY
♀	VENUS
♂	MARS
♃	JUPITER
♄	SATURN
♅	URANUS
♆	NEPTUNE
♇	PLUTO

noticed was that it contained a Grand Trine with planets Pluto, Saturn, and Earth's moon. It also contained Mercury and Neptune in trine with one another.

Additionally, Neptune was in conjunction with mid-heaven. The sign of Scorpio was on his Ascendant. Not only was the sun located in the constellation Pisces, but the earth and Sun were exactly lined up with the Super Galactic Center.

As I interpreted the planetary aspects on his star map, several things caught my attention. Mercury in trine with Neptune means he had the *ability to read the thoughts of others*. I knew for a fact he could do this. The moon in trine with Saturn signifies that he possessed *organizational ability*. This reflects Dawson's ability as an Episcopal priest and Lakota leader of sacred ceremonies. The moon in trine with Pluto indicates that he had the ability of telekinesis. Neptune in conjunction with mid-heaven means that his profession would be *an occult profession*. The sign of Scorpio on the ascendant shows that the individual will *work to improve the status quo and for regeneration*. In Dawson's chart, the earth in relation to the sun was lined up exactly with the longitude of the Super Galactic Center in the first degree of the sign Libra. That his chart interpretations described him so well, forced me to ask the question, "Was it coincidence -- or synchronicity?"

I have addressed here only the highlights in Dawson's chart. There are many more influences that an experienced astrologer could identify by looking at these same charts. Being a novice, and yet being able to recognize that the charts had identified this individual, had a profound effect on me.

Edgar Cayce stated that information from your star map are influences in your life, and that it is helpful to have awareness of these influences. This information gives one insights into opportunities and challenges in one's life.

Astrology can also be used to help in relationships - friends, parents, students, business associates, etc. Having an understanding of the influences upon someone interacting with you gives one additional information to use toward improving your relationships with others.

STAR MAP

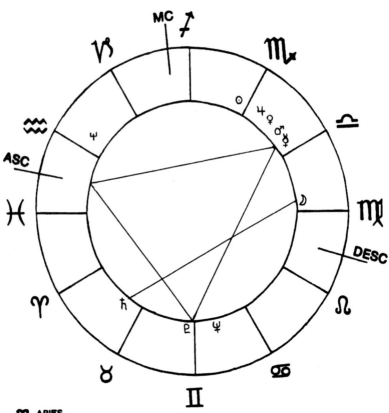

♈ ARIES	
♉ TAURUS	
♊ GEMINI	☽ MOON
♋ CANCER	☉ SUN
♌ LEO	☿ MERCURY
♍ VIRGO	♀ VENUS
♎ LIBRA	♂ MARS
♏ SCORPIO	♃ JUPITER
♐ SAGITTARIUS	♄ SATURN
♑ CAPRICORN	♅ URANUS
♒ AQUARIUS	♆ NEPTUNE
♓ PISCES	♇ PLUTO

164

STAR MAP INFORMATION
for
Agnes Allen Ross

*Each Star Map aspect will be followed by Agnes' sons
written memories in relationship to that aspect.*

Ascendant in Aquarius

You like new ideas and concepts, but it is not easy for
others to convert you to anything. You must form your
own opinions. Once you do form them, you try to
convince everyone else. Try to be tolerant of others'
opinions. Interested in science, math, and social
problems. Great sympathy for the downtrodden.
Equality is your battle cry! You demand that those in
authority must be fair to all. Emotions and emotional
people are difficult for you to understand. Calm and
cool; detached and objective.

Allen: *In the early 1950s, while living in Pine Ridge,
            I noticed my mother's concern for the poorer
            students in her class.*

Kenneth:	*Mom is a product of the nuclear family, where strict adherence to Christian values prevail. Life experiences from the Depression years created thrift-mindedness, tolerance, and empathy for less fortunate persons.*
Duane:	*This aspect led Mom to be a great teacher.*
James:	*Always willing to share opinions or thoughts. Talkative. Concerned for the less fortunate. Education was an equalizer.*

Midheaven in Sagittarius

Good for education and teaching, but whatever your career, you must always feel that you can, at any time, immediately expand your personal horizon through your own efforts. If you ever feel trapped, you will flee to some other pursuit or feel miserable. Because of your ability to see the whole picture, you will gravitate towards positions of leadership, especially with regard to making plans and formulating concepts. An idea person! You are inept, though, at facilitating small details. A very strong sense of justice! This aspect is also good for attracting honors.

Allen:	In 1957, my mother attended summer school in N.A.U., Flagstaff, AZ. We went there to pick her up after the summer session, then we toured Arizona. That was my first recollection of her interest in Education.
	In 1958, my mother won "Teacher of the Year" in South Dakota. I was a senior in high school at that time.
Kenneth:	Mom exhibited a commitment to expand her personal worth through education. She taught children for many years; and, through the praise, adoration, and support of peers, reluctantly elevated herself to principal of Oglala Sioux Community School. She received State and National recognition for outstanding leadership.
Duane:	Mom had a teaching career.
James:	Teacher Corp, Teacher of the Year, Masters Degree, Teacher Supervisor, Tribal Chairperson, Honorary Doctorate degree, College Instructor.

Sun in Scorpio

Scorpios are usually designers, composers, or writers. Intense and complex -- you have extremely strong emotional reactions to situations. Feelings are difficult to verbalize. A tendency to be quiet, a brooder, and a thinker. Seldom angry, but furious and unforgiving when you are. Emotional commitments are total -- never superficial. When emotionally challenged, you lash out and fight back. You love mysteries and the supernatural. A good detective; you like to get to roots of problems and learn what makes others tick. Willful, powerful, and very tenacious!

Allen:
> *My mother never scolded us boys, but once I dropped a jar of peanut butter and broke the jar. My mother scolded me saying, "Now what are we to eat?" She picked the broken glass out of the peanut butter and salvaged what she could for us to eat. This happened when we were living on the farm in Flandreau, SD.*
>
> *I was an adult before I realized my mother had written several books on poetry and children's stories.*

Kenneth: *Mom appears to be very calm, analytical, and thinks through alternatives before action. This quality takes a back seat when established traditions and values conflict with adverse situations, resulting in an emotionally strong, yet firm, reaction.*

Duane: *It takes mom a long time to vocalize what is wanted -- then stands firm.*

James: *Committed to Education - key to any individual's success. Strong belief in God (Christian/Wakan Tanka). Very committed to family. Calm, quiet, but always listening and caring.*

Sun in House Eight

Your life will undergo many interesting and different phases of development. There will be a constant need to grow, change, and evolve. Serious, intent on exploring life's deeper issues. Very responsible about handling possessions and property.

Allen: *My mother was a leader in organizing church functions. Later in 1972, she was elected as the Chairperson of our Tribe.*

Kenneth:	Mom attended the World's Fair in Brussels, Belgium, played tennis, and ran track in her youth. She retired as an active educator to return to the Flandreau tribal community and followed her father's footsteps -- assuming the Chairwomanship of the tribe.
Duane:	Always involved in helping others learn and grow. She herself did grow and prosper because of this.
James:	Mom handled most financial paperwork.

Sun Sextile Moon

(+) Inner emotional balance. Good early upbringing. You flow with events. Your life works smoothly. Accept and enjoy life!
(-) Inner emotional conflict. You noticed parents tensions. You feel you must constantly evolve and challenge yourself.

Allen:	When I was about 4 years old, (while my dad was in World War II) each night before we went to bed my mother would have us boys say a bedtime prayer in which we would end

the prayer by saying, "God, please bring our dad home safe.."

Kenneth: The spiritual and religious upbringing, coupled with rural farm life of hard work, form the personal basis of Mom's strength.

Duane: True.

Sun Conjunct Jupiter

(+) An optimistic, positive attitude toward life. You see and live life on a grand scale. An idealist. Fairness and justice!
(-) Arrogance and conceit. You tend to overdo everything. Extravagant and careless. Self-control and discipline are needed.

Allen: While growing up, I caused my parents much strife by getting myself into problems. My mother would always help me see the good side.

Kenneth: Mom has, as long as I can remember, personified an optimistic outlook on life. An idealist, founded in a hard work ethic, developed a strong sense of self control and discipline.

171

Duane:	More an optimist.

James:	Education is the KEY to a good/comfortable life. Willing to help with projects or talk to students to share her life experiences in the realm of education and Dakota lifestyle.

Sun Opposition Saturn

(+) Patient and self-disciplined. Quiet. Reserved. Dependable. Reliable. Very mature. Extremely concerned with propriety.
(-) Very hard on yourself. Too serious and demanding. Righteous. You feel the world is cold and harsh. Self-critical. Lonely.

Allen:	My mother was Tribal Chairperson in 1972. Also, she retired from the B.I.A. as an Educational Specialist.

Kenneth:	She has extreme patience and is very under-standing for the needs of others.

Duane:	The (+) side is very true. I don't know about the (-) side.

James: Committed to education - key to any individual's success. Strong belief in God (Christian/Wakan Tanka). Very committed to family. Calm, quiet, but always listening and caring.

Sun Trine Pluto

(+) Very strong willed. Powerful. Influential. Charismatic. Leadership potential. Ambition. Life must be lived intensely.
(-) Extreme stubbornness can cause intense personality conflicts and power struggles. Learn to not manipulate others.

Allen: Once, when I was home in 1996, I took my mother to the store to get a few items. The people at the store were so glad to see her -- she greeted them with a joyous response.

Kenneth: Mom is very strong willed, charismatic, worldly, knowledgeable, and uses these personal attributes to influence others and exhibit leadership.

Duane: The (+) side is very true - she shaped many lives.

James: *Strong feelings about education and native peoples, especially the Dakota/Lakota.*

Moon in Virgo

You are serious, but cheerful and need tasks that engage mind and hands. A careful worker, you enjoy making things. Neat, orderly, and very concerned with good health habits. Fastidious to the extreme; messes are immediately cleaned up. Reserved, shy, and very self-critical. Do not be so hard on yourself! You go out of your way to be helpful and useful to others. Practical, reliable, and efficient. At times, a bit of a prude. Methodical and diligent. A simple, frugal, and unemotional lifestyle! This aspect is good for teaching and higher mind activities.

Allen: *While growing up, mother always worked, so it was up to us boys to clean the house. Later, we were taught to cook the supper. She taught us to clean up immediately after ourselves.*

When I was attending college, after I returned from the Army, my mother helped me write a term paper on religion. This was in 1965.

Kenneth: *Many tasks Mom engages in incorporate traditional values. She loves to sew star quilts and pillows with colorful designs. Even today, with failing eyesight, she continues to make star quilts and give them away to grandchildren, children, and friends.*

Duane: *She is very much at ease in this area.*

James: *She likes working with flowers, making star quilts, and sewing. She would immediately clear the table and clean the dirty dishes. In some instances, taking the plates before Dad was done eating. He would tease her about being like her mother (Grandma Allen).*

Moon in House Seven

You need the security and emotional closeness of a deep commitment to a partner. You attract very emotional people to you so that you can learn about your own emotional responses. Partners can be moody, touchy, and irritable. Others react to you.

Allen: *My father was very moody when we were growing up, so we boys learned to stay clear of* him. *My mother says she married her opposite -- she is calm; he is moody.*

Kenneth: *Mom and Dad have been married 59 years, and still show emotional closeness and commitment to one another. Like a pair of geese -- mated for life.*

Duane: *Very true - being married to Dad since 1939.*

James: *Married for over 55 years.*

Moon Trine Saturn

(+) Strict self-control.   Cool logic.   Objectivity. Unemotional decisions.   You like to accept responsibility. Conservative.
(-) Feelings of unworthiness and self-doubt.   Being ashamed of your emotional responses makes it difficult to love others.

Allen: *My mother is very conservative. When we were in grade school, she would make a lot of our clothes. Also, she canned food from our garden every year.*

Kenneth: *Mom has proven to be analytical and;*
            therefore, somewhat conservative. Logic
            prevails in all decision-making activities.

Duane: *Diplomatic.*

James: *Most decisions were not made on emotional*
            levels.

Moon Square Midheaven

(+) Powerful emotions. Others provide encouragement
and emotional support. You get along with the public.
Supportive!
(-) Too passive.   Overly-dependent on others for
support and structure. Over-protective and possessive.
Late-maturing.

Allen: *My mother did not finish college until 1930.*
            She was 27 years old at the time. She did not
            marry until she was 30 years old.

Kenneth: *Mom is the epitome of Love -- for children,*
            grandchildren, friends, relatives, and life in
            general. She is the rock upon which we lean
            for personal support.

Duane: *In the spotlight a lot, but not by her design --*
           others place her there.

James: *Willing to help others in time of need,*
           however, depended a great deal on Dad's
           support and structure. She was always
           concerned about the welfare of all of her
           children, grandchildren, and relatives.

Mercury in Libra

You do not jump to conclusions. All choices are
weighed carefully. A preference for compromises.
Moderation. Ideas and interests must be neat, elegant,
and refined. You speak softly and pleasantly. A born
diplomat. A raconteur of culture and taste.

Allen: *When I was growing up, it seems I was always*
           at ends with my father. My mother had to
           moderate each situation.

Kenneth: *Her soft spoken nature, coupled with born*
           diplomatic characteristics, serve her well in
           counseling others. She is wise and respected
           for her thoughts and compassion.

James: *She was concerned with proper spelling and punctuation, especially with products produced by Indian people.*

Mercury in House Eight

A deep and inquiring mind. A natural psychologist; you are fascinated by exploring the depths of human consciousness. A love of mysteries and the supernatural. Very quiet. Your thoughts are complex and are not easily expressed. Secretive.

Allen: *My mother has been attending the Sun Dance each year for the past 21 years. The last four years she has been the Sun Dance Grandmother at the Black Hills Sun Dance.*

Kenneth: *Mom is a classic, down home psychologist, who seems to intrinsically know where bones are buried in peoples lives, has the ability to get to the core of most, if not all, issues quickly and quietly to assist in problem resolution.*

Duane: *Always looking for more meaning in life.*

James: In her effort to help, she would try to under-
            stand the situation, in particular, the mindset
            of the individuals involved.

            Interested in the unexplainable, but always
            seemed to be looking for some logical explana-
            tion. One of the sayings Dad and I would
            tease her with was, Where did you read that?"
            A couple of times Dad offered some thoughtful
            insight, and she responded by saying,"Where
            did you read that?"

Mercury Conjunct Venus

(+) Talent in arts and crafts. Must be surrounded by
beauty. Ugliness depresses you. Diplomatic. A very
soothing talker.
(-) Vanity. Conceitedness. A tendency to avoid deep
entangling situations. Superficial. Hyper-sensitivity.
Trivial.

Allen: My mother likes to be around nice looking
            subjects. I think this is why she married my
            dad. People have told me, "Your father is so
            handsome. "

180

During her life, my mother had a tendency to be vain. My father would immediately tell her to change the subject.

Kenneth: *Mom, in her own way, is a crafts person -- painting, sewing, cooking new and interesting concoctions.*

Duane: *Mom did quilting and beading.*

James: *She tried her hand at painting, sewing, quilting, gardening, and cooking. She would like to dry corn the old way and make other types of traditional foods , or foods associated with traditional ways.*

She was always in demand for talking to students and was more than willing to oblige.

Mercury Conjunct Mars

(+) You think for yourself. Beliefs are strongly defended. Honest. Self-assured, decisive. Good at debate and repartee.
(-) Rash, impulsive, and anxious. Hot-tempered, nervous, and irritable. Don t take it personally if others disagree. Quarrels!

181

Kenneth:	*Mom will listen and tolerate others, but is a self thinker whose decision, in most matters, is the final decision.*
Duane:	*Exchange of thoughts and ideas are welcomed.*

Mercury Conjunct Jupiter

(+) Multi-faceted interests. Optimistic, open-minded and tolerant. Good at planning and organizing. Loves to travel.
(-) A lack of self-discipline. Sloppy. A tendency to jump to conclusions. Tactless. Clumsy. Negligent and unreliable!

Allen:	*As a youth, my mother and father would always take us camping. Occasionally, we would visit different states.*
Kenneth:	*Mom s interests are definitely multi-faceted, from tennis, hunting, fishing, camping, to touring historic sites and national parks, all of which reveal a love of nature and a quest for greater knowledge.*

Mercury Square Uranus

(+) A love of new and exciting ideas. Impatience with traditional concepts. An independent thinker. A quick, agile mind.
(-) Mental energies tend to scatter and you get nervous and irritable. A shallow thinker. You jump to conclusions. Frenzied!

Kenneth: *As a teacher and school administrator, she explored new and exciting ideas to teach children more effectively. Students of hers from 40 years ago still remember her and respect her. Many still keep in contact or ask about her.*

Duane: *Untrue. Has a lot of patience.*

James: *She worked at Sylvan Lake in the Black Hills, went to Amsterdam, Holland., was a member of a girls athletic sorority at Northern Arizona University at Flagstaff, Arizona., obtained a Masters degree, and was an instructor at various colleges and universities.*

Even though she pursued new ideas and education, she was firmly rooted in many aspects of the Dakota lifestyle/culture.

183

Mercury Square Neptune

(+) A rich and vivid imagination. Sensitivity to others needs. Refined. Creative. An idealist and romantic. Good intuition.

(-) One who distorts the truth. A tendency to escape into your private fantasy world. Avoid drugs and alcohol. Confusion!

Allen: *When we were living on the farm from 1945-50, my Aunt Dorothy passed away, so my mother took care of my cousin during those years.*

In 1996, my brother-in-law was falsely accused of a crime and found guilty. My mother helped us with the bail and getting a lawyer. My brother-in-law got a new trial.

Duane: *Good care giver.*

James: *She was always sensitive to other's needs or problems, and did what she could to help.*

Mercury Trine Pluto

(+) A born investigator. Good at molding the ideas of others. Mind is concerned only with deep matters -- nothing trivial.
(-) A propagandist. Be prepared for resistance when you try to manipulate and control people s thinking patterns. A dictator!

Kenneth: *She is proficient at capturing the positive ideas of others and molding them into realistic, workable processes that she can use in daily activities.*

Duane: *Expresses an idea or thought and others take on the challenge.*

James: *Through education, individuals would be able to have a comfortable living in the dominate society. Always promoted getting a college education.*

Mercury Trine Ascendant

(+) Mind works best when you share ideas with others. Others stimulate your thinking. Many friends and acquaintances.

(-) You hog the conversation when your mind is stimulated. A tendency to love gossip and rumors. Constant idle chatter!

Allen: *At my parents' 57th wedding anniversary, over 1,000 people attended the feed and giveaway.*

Kenneth: *She is constantly sharing her own ideas with others through public speaking, seminars, conferences on Indian history, culture, and traditions.*

Duane: *True.*

James: *She is a very talkative individual, especially on the subjects of education and culture. She occasionally dominates the conversations centered around these subjects.*

Venus in Libra

Friendly, outgoing. You hate to be alone. Beware of compromising yourself to avoid being lonely. Be yourself; don't be what others would like you to be.

Beautiful, graceful, artistic, stylish. Avoid using charm in order to get out of dirty work!

Allen: *I first noticed my mother's fear of being alone, when my father had an emergency operation on his stomach. The doctor said it was touch and go. It was then I heard my mother say that she didn't want my father to go first, because she didn't want to be alone.*

Kenneth: *My mother is very outgoing and will strike up a conversation with almost anyone who will listen to her.*

Duane: *Mother is friendly and outgoing.*

James: *Indian name was Wihopa - Pretty Woman. She had a beautiful inner self that was warm and caring. Through her being an educator, she sought to help others.*

Venus in House Eight

Vivid and intense sensual self-expression. Relationships are intensely confrontative and full of feeling. Being too possessive of others will cause resentment. You choose relationships in which both of you must be changed. You like to share.

Kenneth:	*Mom avoids confrontation, but will diplomatically state her position on most matters.*
Duane:	*I ve recognized confrontation in her marriage.*
James:	*She was very concerned about the welfare of her family. This caused some friction with her daughters-in-law.*

Venus Conjunct Mars

(+) Strong emotional responses. A great need to give and receive affection. Very sexy. Strong creative drive. Lusty enthusiasm!
(-) A mix of love/hate feelings in relationships. Stormy feelings about the opposite sex. Hot-and-cold affairs. Infidelity.

Allen:	*My mother always cared for her students. She had a need to help them beyond just the classroom exercises.*

Kenneth: Mom openly gives affection to others, espe-
            cially to her main man, Dad. She loves to play
            mind games and tease with a unique sense of
            humor.

Venus Conjunct Jupiter

(+) Very sociable. Generous, warm and affectionate.
friendly. Fully of honesty and integrity. A comfortable
life. Can be rich.
(-) Self-discipline is lacking. Overly self-indulgent. A
tendency to be lazy and gain weight. You always
overdo everything!

Allen: While living at Pine Ridge, both my parents
            were employed. We lived in government
            housing. So, by reservation standards, we
            were rich and had a comfortable life.

            During middle age, my mother had a problem
            with being overweight.

Kenneth: Mom has placed a premium of high value on
            the pursuit of education for all family members
            and has financially assisted sons and grand-
            children in pursuing higher education goals.

James: She was generous, warm, and affectionate.
            Friendly and caring.

Venus Opposition Saturn

(+) Serious. Quiet. Restrained and shy. Relationships must be based on reliability and responsibility. Loyal and dutiful.
(-) Cold. Detached emotionally. You feel unworthy to be loved. Indifferent. Lonely. Extremely shy. Lacking self-confidence.

Kenneth: Mom places significant value in demonstrated
            action of family who show, by their actions, a
            sense of personal growth to be reliable and
            responsible for their actions.

James: It seems that her marriage encompassed
            certain responsibilities that she had and
            certain responsibilities that Dad had. She was
            the homemaker and took care of the paperwork.
            Dad did most of the cleaning, maintenance,
            and yard work.

Venus Square Uranus

(+) Relationships must be with unusual, exciting and interesting people. Happily unconventional, you must do your own thing.
(-) Relationships are very unstable and changeable. Undependable and irresponsible. Unable to honor deep, close commitments.

Allen: *While growing up in our household, occasion-ally my mother would get fed up with my father telling her what to do; She would do what she wanted over his objections.*

Kenneth: *Mom has shown tolerance and amazement in her ability to permit her sons to do their own thing, especially when it comes to the eldest son, Brother Chuck, who on occasion is mentally on a different psychological plane.*

James: *She worked at Sylvan Lake in the Black Hills, went to Amsterdam, Holland., was a member of a girls athletic sorority at Northern Arizona University at Flagstaff, Arizona, obtained a Masters degree, and was an instructor at various colleges and universities.*

Venus Square Neptune

(+) A romantic imagination. Artistic creativity. Idealistic and unselfish in relationships. You prefer to love platonically.
(-) You tend to avoid the harsh realities in relationships until things are completely out of hand. Many disillusionments!

Allen: *Mom was always lovey dovey toward Dad, but he never responded, at least not in public.*

Kenneth: *Mom's romantic imagination is personified in the poetry she has written and published.*

James: *Romantic in the sense that formal education was the answer to having a good life; and, through education, the culture would be preserved and passed on to other generations.*

Venus Trine Pluto

(+) Relationships must be alive, intense and evolving for you to remain interested. A deep and total commitment to another.

(-) Overly jealous and overly possessive of others. Destructive, manipulative, confrontative relationships. Demanding!

Allen: *During my life, I've noticed that no matter what people thought about my dad, my mother thought he was her one and only. She is totally committed to him. He could do no wrong in her eyes.*

Kenneth: *Mom understands only too well that relationships evolve -- highs and lows. She has nurtured positive relationships and advocated abandonment when all options have failed.*

James: *Over 55 years of marriage.*

Mars in Libra

A strong sense of cooperation. A willingness to compromise. A need to get along and be with others, although sometimes competitive. Fair-minded. Aware of injustices. You see both sides of issues and questions. You tend to waiver between two choices.

Allen:	Once, while my mother was Chairperson of our Tribe, one of her cousins by the name of Gordon, was giving her a hard time. Maybe he was jealous, I don't know. But anyway, during Christmas, my mother took him and his family gifts and a cake. Gordon s wife, who knew what he had been doing to my mother, cried and couldn't thank her.
Kenneth:	Mom is a person who truly believes in the concept that the nuclear family must cooperate with one another in pursuit of common positive goals.
Duane:	Mother has a strong sense of sharing and getting along with others.
James:	She always tried to help. She weighed the options and tried to come up with a good solution for everyone.

Mars in House Eight

Everything is done with great intensity. You drive yourself very hard physically. Learn moderation. You are not as indefatigable as you think you are. Your strong, powerful desires can lead to conflicts with others. Learn to share.

Kenneth: *Mom has exhibited, through personal action, that goal achievement is at the expense of personal inconvenience and physical limitations.*

Mars Conjunct Jupiter

(+) Optimistic and buoyant. Energetic and active. Athletic ability. Exuberance. An innate sense of good timing. Good fortune!
(-) A tendency to take foolish chances. You feel as if nothing can ever go wrong. A hasty and sloppy worker. Accident-prone.

Allen: *Although I didn't witness my mother's athletic abilities, members of her family told me that she was a great athlete in running, tennis, and basketball. I do remember once, when my brother fell into the flooded creek below our house, I ran and told my mother, who was in the house. She ran, jumped the fence, and leaped from a high bank into the swollen creek water. She pulled my brother to safety.*

Kenneth:	Throughout her life, Mom has remained physically active, even to her own consternation. Like the time she almost burnt the house down while trying to cook, do laundry, and keep track of Dad.
James:	She played basketball, was a good runner, member of a college women's athletic sorority, bowler, and liked to dance.

Mars Square Uranus

(+) Restless and unconventional. Independent. Must be free to be yourself at all costs. Daring. Life must be unique and exciting.
(-) Disruptive and unsettling. Rash and headstrong. Impulsiveness puts you in danger. May be accident-prone. Rebellious!

Kenneth:	Mom's view of life is that it is exciting to see the changes in technology and all other aspects of total societal changes in the past 50 years or so.
James:	Independent, headstrong when it came to the welfare of family members.

Mars Square Neptune

(+) An idealist. A need for self-denial. Compassion and sympathy for those in trouble. You are giving and unselfish.
(-) Easily discouraged. Low energy. Unaggressive. Defeatist attitude. Beware escaping reality through drugs or delusion!

Allen: *My wife was in an auto accident in 1993. Unable to work, she was offered a medical retirement; but, before she could receive her retirement, she needed to repay a portion of her retirement. My mother helped her with the settlement.*

Kenneth: *These traits personify my mother.*

James: *She was always sensitive to other's needs or problems, and did what she could to help.*

Mars Trine Pluto

(+) Strong-willed. Positive drive and ambition. You like to have power and to use it responsibly. A formidable opponent!

(-) Manipulation and control over others. Bad-tempered. Violent tendencies. Underhanded and unethical tactics. Dictatorial!

Allen: *My mother continued her education and received her Masters degree in 1958.*

Kenneth: *Mom has demonstrated, throughout her life, a self controlled ambition to improve her lot in life through self denial, hard work, sharing, and generosity to others.*

James: *She possessed a strong will and a positive drive, as shown by her achievements.*

Mars Trine Ascendant

(+) Self-reliant. Courageous and daring. Aggressive and independent. Very competitive. Sports & physical contact. Energetic.
(-) Quarrelsome and domineering. Defensive and bad-tempered. Uncooperative. Resentful. Hostile. Avoid danger and accidents.

Allen: *While we boys were participating in high school athletics, my mother would attend many of the games to support our team.*

Kenneth: *Mom's independence was exhibited in her pursuit of a college degree, when she left for school and arranged to have Dad take care of us boys for over a year.*

James: *Teacher Corp, Teacher of the Year, Masters Degree, Teacher Supervisor, Tribal Chairperson, Honorary Doctorate degree, College Instructor. She played basketball, was a good runner, member of a college women's athletic sorority, bowler, and liked to dance.*

Jupiter in Libra

You are good at balancing and judging issues, but you tend to be indecisive about making up your mind. Art interests demand expansiveness and elegance. Relationships are important: you learn about yourself through others. Fair play and justice!

Kenneth: *Mom's art interests are expansive not expensive, but highly practical in nature.*

Duane: *Mother is good at balancing issues.*

Jupiter in House Eight

Many major but positive psychological changes. Each change brings new understanding, experience, and knowledge. You like to share and cooperate. Relationships bring money and/or material advantage. A good understanding of human nature. Wasteful.

Allen: *My mother has many friends. One, in particular, I remember was a fellow teacher. This lady was a black lady and was from Texas. Her name is Mrs. Lucille Abbott. It was hard for Mrs. Abbott to find work. She eventually located work in the B.I.A. and was assigned to Pine Ridge Agency. She worked and sent her money home to her family. She finally retired and moved back to Texas. I think she still writes to my mother.*

Kenneth: *Mom's ability to capture the positive value of previous experiences and apply feasible solutions to new situations has been shown through in her decision making.*

James: *Mom went through some changes in relationship to how she strove to help individuals through education — bi-lingual teacher, teacher supervisor, teacher corp, lecturer, and preservation of language and culture.*

Jupiter Opposition Saturn

(+) Patient and willing to work hard. You know how to balance idealism and practicality. Good business ability. Perseverance.
(-) Mentally very restless. Not content. Activities not satisfying. Goals not reached. You feel others block your growth.

Allen: *Over the years, I've caused my mother many heart aches and grief. I'm sorry for that, but it was my mother's patience and support that helped me attain my education. Thank you, Mother.*

Kenneth: *These traits have been exhibited throughout her life.*

James: *Summer school - Masters degree. 30 years of government service. Tribal Chairperson.*

Jupiter Square Uranus

(+) An optimist. You project positive energy. Lucky breaks come to you out of the blue. Tolerant, liberal, and inventive.

(-) Impatient. Unwilling to put up with restrictions. Playfully disruptive. Immature belief: everything old is bad.

Allen: *My mother has stated that she never had to apply for a job. The jobs just sort of came to her.*

Kenneth: *Mom's attitude is that anything, any goal is achievable through hard work and perseverance.*

James: *She was always positive about the future. Positive about life.*

Jupiter Square Neptune

(+) Idealistic, optimistic and romantic. A dreamer. strong interests in spirituality and religion. Sensitive. Charitable.
(-) You live in your fantasies too much. Inflated expectations will lead to disillusionment. You should never ever gamble!!!!

Allen: *My mother grew up as a Christian. She served the church faithfully until her boys started Sun Dancing. Now, she is totally involved in the Sun Dance.*

Kenneth: *As long as I can recall, Mom has been the spiritual/religious foundation in our development.*

James: *Very religious person. Interested in the spirituality of others and unexplainable occurences.*

Jupiter Trine Pluto

(+) A strong drive to be a success. Powerful and charismatic. A catabolic agent for positive and creative change. Good leader.
(-) Impatient, unwilling to let others have their way; you will be seen by them as a threat and they will try to block you.

Allen: *My mother was a good leader. She was able to show the people how to accomplish things, rather than dictate her leadership.*

Kenneth: *Personal and professional respect have evolved because of maximizing positive astrological aspects.*

James: *She provided a calm, positive leadership role in the family, relative to emphasizing the importance of getting a college education. She had heart problems, but would not quit working until I graduated from college. Therefore, I went year round and finished college in three years.*

Saturn in Taurus

Complete freedom makes you ill at ease. You must have a firm, secure foundation in life in order to feel comfortable. You do not adapt easily and tend to fear the new. You need plenty of emotional support to cure your fear of not having enough!

Allen: *My dad has always provided a secure environment for my mother -- in her work, home, and personal life. He has been her protector, as well as her guide.*

Kenneth: *Mom has committed herself to be an honorable, dedicated, loving partner through her marriage. Complete freedom is not an option. Life must be shared.*

James: She developed a firm foundation with being
            married for over 55 years. She depended on
            Dad's strength to support her.

Saturn in House Two

Cautious and conservative about money and any other
resource. You are afraid that there will not be enough.
You fear unexpected shortages.   Thrift.   A careful
planner. You prefer to work hard for what you get. you
may become stingy and miserly.

Allen: *My mother grew up in the Depression days;
            therefore, she is very conservative and thrifty.
            She is always saving something and taught us
            boys to appreciate Salvation Army-type stores.*

Kenneth: *Money management has been exemplified by
            caution and conservation. Saving for a rainy
            day and future investment benefits is an
            innate quality.*

James: *She took care of most financial matters. She
            was organized and prepared for contingencies.
            She was willing to work for what she got and
            believed this to be a goal that everyone should*

pursue. Through education, one could obtain a comfortable living. She did not like the idea of living on welfare, or expecting/demanding the tribe to provide things for people.

Uranus in Capricorn

Uranus was in Capricorn from 1904 to 1912 and is there from 1988 to 1996. These generations have practical solutions for changing society's attitudes to customs and traditions and authority structures. These changes will be permanent.

Allen: *Through personal example and self expression, my mother has exemplified how one should live in these days of changing attitudes to customs/traditions.*

Kenneth: *Respect, honor, and reliance on the innate, intrinsic knowledge, skills, and abilities of women will create a more balanced societal and political structure that yields positive benefits.*

James: *Has assisted granddaughter in utilizing teaching materials she developed four decades ago for today's classroom.*

Uranus in House Twelve

You tend to suppress your need to be an individual. You try to live up to the expectations of others. Only your imagined fears are holding you back from the exciting life-style that you crave. Compulsive behavior and sudden actions!

Allen: *My mother has stated that her supervisor wanted her to continue her education, so she could receive a Master's degree. This she did in 1958.*

Kenneth: *Group dynamics and team work yields long lasting and easier acceptability of decisions and direction.*

Uranus Opposition Neptune

(+) The ability to experiment with consciousness and spiritual matters in general. Very idealistic and anti-materialistic!
(-) A genuine fear of being confused about what is real and what is not. Fear and confusion about the occult and mysticism.

Allen: *My mother has had many an opportunity to participate in the Sweat Lodge and Sun Dance. On one occasion, I heard her tell a group of students that a spirit plate was food for the little animals, even though she knew the food was for the spirits. This is a rare example of her confusion about mystical things and her need to present mysticism in a non-threatening manner.*

Kenneth: *Adherence to traditional values of sharing and generosity in the sacred hoop yields positive returns if practiced routinely throughout life.*

James: *Being raised in a Christian family, I believe she experienced some fear/confusion about Wakan Tanka. However, having a firm foundation in the Dakota life/culture, she reconciled any conflicts.*

Neptune in Cancer

Neptune was in Cancer from 1902 to 1916. This generation tended to over-idealize the home, the past, and other traditional values. This fostered various isolationist and ultra-nationalistic movements throughout the world. Super-conservatives!

Allen: My mother has emphasized the need to be thrifty and conservative within the home and on personal matters.

Kenneth: Home is where the heart is, and traditional family values practiced routinely result in positive growth.

James: Mom is a fairly conservative person. This may come from her upbringing in a somewhat traditional Dakota home.

Neptune in House Six

Feelings of inadequacy and self-doubt make you think you always have to give in to others or serve them. Build your sense of self-confidence. Your body is very sensitive to outside influences. Emotional problems lead to illness and allergies. This aspect is good for aiding those who are less fortunate.

Allen: My mother has contended that a good wife must serve her husband. This was the traditional Lakota way, but times are changing. * See last chapter on the analysis of the female medicine bundle.

209

Kenneth: *A positive sense of self worth has balanced the scale, where no and defined limits of helpfulness are exercised; with the concept that one needs to maximize their own potential, rather than be constantly a welfare recipient.*

James: *Mom has some sort of allergies. Her nose is constantly running during certain times of the year.*

Pluto in Gemini

Pluto was in Gemini from 1882 to 1912. When Pluto was in the sign Gemini, the world experienced profound breakthroughs in the ability of people to communicate with each other. From the automobile to the telephone and air travel: a global community!

Kenneth: *Communication, open, honest, truthful is a key to positive relationships.*

James: *Teacher Corp, Teacher of the Year, Masters Degree, Teacher Supervisor, Tribal Chairperson, Honorary Doctorate degree, College Instructor.*

Pluto in House Five

When you have fun, you do so totally, as if your life were at stake. Putting everything on the line gets your adrenaline surging. Winning is so important that fun times often turn into fights, arguments, and disputes. A real one-track-mind. This aspect stipulates that the first child will change the mothers life on a psychological level. Also there may be an issue of survival with the 1st child.

Allen: *The first child of Wihopa (Agnes Allen Ross) wrote the best selling book on the Psychology of American Indian Ceremonialism. Agnes first child was about five years old when he drowned, but he was brought back to life by artificial respiration.*

Kenneth: *Having fun is a key part of balancing stress and results that balance one s life.*

James: *Winning at life was very important to her. Through education and spirituality, she believed an individual could achieve success in living a comfortable life. She did what she could to help her family achieve such a goal. She continues to help her grandchildren in their pursuits as well.*

"If a Star Map of all twelve constellations
is superimposed over the Earth with the
Pole Star placed over the terrestrial North
Pole, we have a celestial clock making one
revolution daily. The noon point of that
Star Map would be the Great Pyramid of
Giza. (Thousands of years ago, Egypt was
known as the land of Khem. The Khema
were a group of seven major stars known
today as the Pleiades.) Now if the Star
Map is placed with the Khema over the
land of Khem "Egypt" - specifically,
directly above the apex of the Great
Pyramid - then Taurus falls over the
Taurus mountains of southern Turkey;
Ursa Major, the Great Bear, rambles over
Russia; the head of Draco the Dragon coils
up over China; Orion over Iran and Iraq;
Aries the Ram over Rome; and Capricorn
(identified with the god Pan) falls over
Panama, Panuco, and Mayapan (old name
for Yucatan); and Aquila the Eagle spans
the United States. The analogies are
obvious and quite impressive. This is one
of the clearest examples of the law "As
Above, So Below."

Moira Timms, 1994

212

A FEMALE MEDICINE BUNDLE
AND THE FEMININE ENERGY

As I was reviewing the comparisons between my mother's star map and her life's experiences, I was not surprised that the interpretation of my mother's star map were identical to her life's experiences, but I had this feeling that something was missing. As I mentally reviewed her life, I realized that she had been a fore-runner for women's achievements. Her accomplish-ments were done in a time when it was very difficult, if not impossible, for women to achieve. A quick review of her experiences.

1920's   1st place in the foot races at the 4th of July celebrations, even winning over the boys.

1929   1st in her family to attend college.

1931   One of the 1st American Indian Women to graduate from college.

1938-41	1st Dakota bilingual teacher to use music as a teaching method.
	1st Dakota teacher to use experiential teaching methods (learn by doing).
1950	1st Pre-Kindergarten teacher (position established because of bilingual ability).
1958	1st Dakota Woman to receive South Dakota Teacher of the year.
1958	One of the 1st Dakota Women to receive a Masters Degree.
1960	1st Educational Specialist to supervise the Kindergarten teachers reservation-wide (Pine Ridge Reservation).
1963	Helped organize 1st Oglala Sioux Conference on Indian Education.
1968	Helped establish 1st college on Pine Ridge Reservation.

1972	1st woman Tribal Chairperson Flandreau Santee Sioux, United Sioux Tribes of South Dakota
1974	1st Dakota Woman to serve on the South Dakota State Manpower/Planning Service Council.
1975	1st Dakota woman to serve on the South Dakota State Board of Cultural Preservation.
1980	1st Dakota woman to receive Honorary Doctorate from Oglala Lakota College.
1996	1st Dakota woman to receive a Lifetime Achievement Award from the South Dakota N.I.E.A. Host Committee.

After reviewing my mother's achievements, I realized that she was a predecessor for the Women's Liberation Movement, but I did not recognize it in her Star Map. So, I called my astrologer and asked how does one recognize the feminine energy in a star map. My astrologer said that

Scorpio, Virgo, and Capricorn were feminine energies. All three are prominent in my mother's star map. Next, the astrologer said that the Planet Uranus represents Liberation, and that in my mother's star map Uranus was located in Capricorn – meaning a Liberation of the Feminine Energy. Also, my mother's sun was in Scorpio, meaning she would be a transformer of the feminine energy. This is exactly what I was looking for. My mother was a predecessor for the women's liberation movement (the feminine energy), because of who she is and what she has done. She was able to provide many opportunities for women that followed. Women would now be able to follow her footsteps as a teacher, administrator, tribal chairperson, and leader within their community. Now I had a better understanding of why Dawson No Horse said she was The Keeper of the Female Medicine Bundle. The Bundle was not for healing of the physical, but rather for healing of the feminine psychological energy. Realizing that astro energy is not limited to aiding one person, I decided to explore what effect the feminine energy was having world wide during my mother's life time.

1917   Bolshevik Revolution communists declare equality of the sexes.

1920   Women's suffrage (U.S. 19th Amendment) ratified.

1932	Amelia Earhart, 1st woman to fly across Atlantic Ocean.
1935	Maria Montessori's instructional techniques expand.
1940's	Eleanor Roosevelt was an advocate for women.
1955	Rosa Parks refused to give her seat on a Public Bus to a white man.
1963	Betty Friedan writes The Feminine Mystique the book ignites a Women's Liberation Movement.
1963	1st woman in space Valentina V. Tereshkova.
1970 s	Women's Liberation Movement expands
1973	Roe v. Wade, states may not prohibit abortions.
1981	1st woman on Supreme Court, Sandra Day O'Conner.

1988	1st Islamic woman Prime Minister, Benazir Bhutto.
1993	1st woman U.S. Attorney General, Janet Reno.
1996	U.S. Supreme Court orders all-male, Virginia military institute to admit women.
1997	1st women's basketball league, WNBA.

I decided to explore the reason for the increase of the feminine energy. Carl Jung, noted psychologist, stated that when a system is out of balance, that system would reach a point where it would seek its own balance. This process is known as entropy. The world has been dominated by the male energy. We have been living in a left brain (masculine) dominated society. The system is now experiencing entropy. The following is taken from my book Mitakuye Oyasin:

"The research that has been done on brain hemisphericy states that each side of the brain is dominant in different modes of thought: the left is logical, linear, verbal, abstract, sequential, serial, and masculine thought. The right is instinctive, wholistic, non-verbal, concrete, random, spatial, and feminine thought. Barbara Vitale, in her book Unicorns are Real: A Right -Brained Approach to Learning, offers these listings of the brain modes of thought, as well as the skills which follow.

Skills associated with left hemispheric specialization include following directions, reading, writing, detail, reciting, phonetics, and listening. I have been master of ceremonies at many wacipis (pow-wows) throughout the country. I remember one time in Denver, the area where the dancers came in and out of the pow-wow arena was becoming plugged with non-Indians who kept blocking the flow of traffic. As master of ceremonies, I asked them to keep the area clear, but the request went unheard. Realizing that the majority of non-Indians are left-brain dominate, I quickly put up a sign that read, "Keep this area clear." As soon as the non-Indians saw the sign, they quickly cleared the area, thus enabling the dancers to go in and out of the arena unhampered.

The right side of the brain also has specialized skills associated with it: creativity, math computation, haptic awareness, music, artistic ability, color sensitivity, visualization.

My research into brain hemisphericy indicated that modern society and our school systems stress the skills and modes of thinking more on the left side of the brain than on the right. Consequently, I learned to place emphasis on books and libraries as the sources of all knowledge.

By contrast, in traditional D/Lakota culture, any time a person wanted knowledge or information, he attended a ceremony and requested that information from an iyeska (interpreter for the spirits or Holy Man). I learned that in a traditional D/Lakota manner, if one wanted to gain knowledge, he tied an eagle feather onto the spot where the handle and the bowl of the pipe meet. When you use the sacred pipe in a ceremony in this way, you receive knowledge.

In reviewing brain hemisphericy, I concluded that the right hemisphere forms the doorway to the collective unconscious. Any time a person wants information, it's in the collective unconscious portion of the mind.

A hundred years ago D/Lakota people did not have a written language. They did not have books. Any time they wanted knowledge or information, they asked for it ceremonially from the iyeska (interpreter for the spirits or Holy Man). Ceremonies were used to find cures for ailments, to interpret dreams, to find things that had been lost, and to look at your past in order to understand your purpose in life as revealed in your vision quest.

Continuing my research, I discovered a book by Thomas Blakeslee entitled

The Right Brain. He related that there were different right-brain methods of problem solving. One example was dream analysis. He asked, "Did you ever go to bed at night with a question on your mind? Then wake with the answer or dream the answer?"

A further example he gave was meditation. One kind is mindfulness, where you allow any thought to penetrate consciousness, think on it, then let it go. Another thought comes up, you think on it, then let it go. Blakeslee said that creative think tanks around the world use such methods for problem solving.

Fasting to help solve problems was another example put forth by Blakeslee. He stated that Plato, who produced the finest school of philosophy in western civilization, required that his students fast for ten days before they took a test. To me, this is almost the same as traditional D/Lakotas receiving answers while fasting in the vision quest.

Also in the traditional D/Lakota

way, you were not allowed to question the elders. You were taught to listen. You were never allowed to ask the question, "Why?" That's the way I grew up. But this traditional concept came into conflict when I went to boarding school. If you didn't raise your hand and ask, "Why?" -- questioning everything -- you usually ended up with a D or an F.

About ten years ago, I attended a workshop in Denver called *Balancing the Brain*. The presenter, Dr. William Boast, told the participants at the beginning of his workshop, "I'm not going to allow you to ask any questions in this workshop. I'm also going to frown upon anybody who takes notes at any great length." He continued, "For every question you have, the answer is right here." And he pointed to his head. He said, "Man has to begin reorganizing his thinking, and you might as well start now while you're in this workshop!" He added, "Don't worry if you have questions. The answers will come to you in their own time." I found these ideas reinforcing to the traditional D/Lakota way, making me feel good about the workshop.

In reading a book on Indian education, *Speaking of Indians* by Ella Deloria, I discovered that a traditional D/Lakota mode of educating was through example. Children learned by someone setting an example for them. For instance, when a young boy came of age, his uncle or grandfather usually took him along on the hunt. The boy followed along and just watched. Maybe a whole year went by. He was taken along on many different activities, and only later allowed to attempt the task at hand.

Blakeslee commented that a delivery method allowing the right side of the brain to function as a doorway to the collective unconscious is that of learning through discovery. By permitting the child to discover his own answer, his understanding and retention of that experience are much greater. Once again, I was thrilled by this explanation; it was exactly the same as the traditional D/Lakota way of learning through precept and example.

Other examples of right-brain activities offered by Blakeslee were visual aids, diagrams, charts, key words, and phrases. When I came across the word phrases, I remembered in a story of Jesus, based on the Edgar Cayce Readings compiled by Clifford P. Owens that the only time the Master wrote, he used a phrase to teach the people. Was Jesus a right-hemispheric dominant person? He wrote no term papers or theses. As a matter of fact, his occupation was that of a carpenter, one which largely utilizes right-brain functions.

Respect for each individual is a traditional D/Lakota value. In the old way, when a woman married a man, she did not take his name but kept her own name. If they had four children, the children did not take the man's name either. They each received their own names. The common name was the *tiyospaye* or clan name. But then somebody came across the ocean and said, "Don't believe that, you Indian women. When you get married you gotta take the man's name." Now you're Mrs. Chuck Ross, and you'd better obey! Once again, I could see how these two examples are related to brain hemisphericy, the left side being masculine in its expression and the right side being feminine in its expression."

The Dakota People have always recognized and honored the feminine energy. Traditionally, our nation was matriarchal. The woman ruled in the home; she made the Tipi, owned the Tipi, and was boss in the Tipi. However, she did not vocalize any orders. The husband was the spokesperson. If she wanted to give a directive, she would tell her husband

and then he would give the order. This provided for a balance between the male and female energies. Also, there was a division of labor by the sexes. This was not sexist discrimination. By working in cohesion they provided a harmonious whole. Any children born unto the couple would follow the mother's line (tribe). The mother's sisters are also the children's mother. Therefore, the children of sisters were not cousins, but brothers and sisters. Traditionally, Dakota children were never in want of care. The children were never spanked when disciplined. The discipline was controlled by an imaginary character. In Dakota culture, this character was called the chi chi man. In the Hopi culture, the character was the soyoko kachinas. The Hopi women built the Adobe homes and also owned them. Hopi kinship was matriarchal. The women were keepers of the fields, homes, and livestock. Women preserved the sacred ritual objects of the clans. All children belong to the mother's clan.

The men worked the fields, carried burdens, and dominated religion and politics.

David Hurst Thoms writing in *The Native Americans: an Illustrated History* states that,

"Among the Hotinonsonni (Iroquois) their kin relations was determined through the female line. Each long house under a single roof, lived the women and their children. They all belonged to a single matrilineal clan, presided over by a mother, the oldest woman. Over the door of the long house were depictions of the clan's original ancestor. The Iroquois clans were named after the first ancestor: The Eagle, The Heron, The Wolf, The Beaver, etc. Everything in Iroquois society, including the long house belonged to women. The clan mothers appointed and dismissed all councillor-chiefs. Men left home and moved in with the wife. Women did the field work; men were the hunters and warriors."

If the Indians go to war without the consent of the great women, the mothers of the clans; the Great Spirit will not prosper them in war, but will cause them and their efforts to end in disgrace. John Adlum, 1794 (traveling among the Seneca).

A Santee Dakota legend states that "if the women did not agree with a decision to go to war, the tiyospaye mothers would paint a rock red and throw it in the middle of the men's council meeting. When this happened, there was no more discussion on the issue, the women's resolution was final."

Thoms goes on to say that among the Algonquian people of the Great Lakes, the relatives of unmarried women defended their right to regulate their own sexual activity on the grounds that women were masters of their own bodies. What was once denounced as wanton by early European observers is now praised as sexually liberated.

Richard White writing in *The Native Americans: an Illustrated History* also states,

"The difference that most often surprised Europeans in the 17th and 18th centuries was that they frequently encountered women where they expected to confront men."

When different societies with different roles collide, each initially tends to see the other not only as different, but as unnatural.

In Dakota spirituality, the earth was considered feminine and the people called her Mother Earth. The hero archetype was also considered feminine and is known as the White Buffalo Calf Maiden. Almost all tribes had a female as their Hero Archetype. The Hopi have Corn Mother, the Navajo have Changing Women, the Taos have Deer Mother, and the Iroquois had the Three Sisters. Cherokee have corn women and Apache have White Painted Mother. In *The Portable Jung* by Joseph Campbell, he states that in the early Christian church, the Trinity was symbolized by a dove named Sophia, which was a feminine entity!

How did modern man become so out of balance in the way he views the world? Was it when he invented a written language? Or was it when he invented time references (calendar/clock)? Or was it when he invented money (which have lead to economic theories)? All of these inventions utilize left brain modes of thought. Consequently, we live in a left brain dominant world (masculine oriented).

According to Rayna Green, author of *Women in American Indian Society*, information about American Indian women was first documented by the European white male chauvinist, who possessed religious bigotry. Therefore, a clear picture of early American Indian women did not emerge. The truth is that upon the arrival of the European, native women enjoyed suffrage, sexual liberation, social status of matriarchy, and economic independence (since they did the work, they owned the produce/products). At the completion of Dakota ceremonies, we say *Mitakuye Oyasin*, which in its spiritual content means everything is related. Traditionally, all planting societies were matriarchal and all hunting societies were patriarchal. After the Lakota acquired the horse, their culture slowly changed from that of a planting society to that of the hunter. But the respect for the feminine has remained among our people. According to the psychic prophet Edgar Cayce, "Entropy of the masculine and feminine energy would begin in 1933. At that time, souls of an androgynous nature would enter the new born bodies here on earth." This may be the reason for male bodies acting more feminine and female bodies acting masculine nowadays. This is good because it provides a balance of the Anima (female) within the male, and the Animus (male) within the female. Edgar Cayce states that the influx of the androgynous souls would continue for 100 years. These androgynous bodies will be the next root race to enter earth's plane, and they will create the millennium of peace of which the Bible speaks.

Betty Friedan, author of *The Feminine Mystique*, stated in the October 1963 edition of her book that the reason the Equal Rights Amendment was not ratified by the States owes more the Republican Party and

President Reagan's lobbying efforts against it than to an anti-woman campaign. (They feared an undermining of their economic policy which was to give the money to the rich. The money would then filter down to the poor, rather than give money to the poor, so the poor could help themselves. Friedan goes on to say that the women's movement has to move beyond the male model of equality. The movement had transcended its necessary reaction against the Feminine Mystique. Now the movement needed a second stage, a model of equality encompassing female experience. It needed to come to terms with work and the family. Ms. Friedan goes on to say that as female values begin to be shared by the male, she wondered are the values of men changing? Those young men who carry their little babies so proudly in their backpacks to the supermarket? Those men now suffering the mid-life crises? If men don't want to die at an early age from their leading killer, cardiac arrest, they must develop the flexibility and sensitivity to their own feelings, the attunement to life, that has been considered up to now feminine.

This is something that the American Indian society had figured out long ago and was practicing when the Europeans landed in North America.

"It is best to treat women with consideration and respect, for they are the ones who will care for you in your infancy and in your old age."

Chief He Dog, 1880

"Our mothers, wives, and daughters have been the keepers of our culture. They more than anyone in our nation deserve our respect."

Ehanamani aka Dr. A.C. Ross

"A nation is not conquered until the hearts of its women are on the ground."

Blackfeet Men's Society

"Women are, in fact, the moral salvation of our people."

Ohiyesa aka Dr. Charles Eastman

John Van Auken, in his book *The End Times*, interpreting Daniels 3rd vision in Daniel 9:20-24, states that, "Sometime between 1996 and 1999 will host the return of the Messiah." Edgar Cayce, psychic prophet, said the Master will return in 1998, Nostradamus implies 1999. Futurist Gordon Michael Scallion states that, "in 1998 a child will be born who will eventually emerge as the Master Teacher. This event has been heralded by the comet, Hale-Bopp", he says, "and is called the "Blue Star" by the Hopi and the "Heart of the White Buffalo" by the Sioux." The White Buffalo constellation represents the White Buffalo maiden. This energy is a feminine energy. Will the next master teacher be a female?"

Since we know not where the master teacher child will be born, it is imperative that all who will be parents in 1998 prepare themselves. All women should treat their bodies with respect. All men should be considerate and helpful to their wives. A great event is about to happen. Above all remember your spirituality, whichever you choose, for there is only one creator.

IN CONCLUSION

We have come a long way in the treatment of women, but we still have a long way to go. Two incidents which happened this past year immediately come to mind. An acquaintance of mine was attending the local college on her reservation in South Dakota. She is married and they have two children. She asked her unemployed husband to babysit the children while she attended classes. He refused, saying, "Sioux men don't babysit." Then, when she received her grant money, he wanted her to give him some so he could "go party with the boys."

The second incident occurred on a reservation in Arizona. This lady was stopped by the Tribal police, she was placed in the squad car while he "checked her out." Finding nothing, he told her she was free to go. On her way back to her car, the officer called, saying, "Come back here and look where you were sitting in the squad car, there's a bag of marijuana." He arrested her for possession of the drug. Later it was learned that the officer had been trying to date her and she had refused him, so this is how he "would show her; she can't get away with what she did to him." Obviously, the officer had planted the marijuana. It is time to "grow up" men. It is time to get real. Life is not a game where you play with people's lives as if they have no feelings. What I mean by "grow up" is to educate yourself as to the real history and culture of our people. We need to eliminate the European stereotypes of our culture. We live in changing times, but a model based on the Matriarchal clan system is the answer. In that system, each member of the family contributes their share. If men find this a little hard to accept, then you are on the right path. In Psychology, this path is called Individuation. Individuation is the process of becoming whole (growing up). Becoming whole is completed when a person consciously comes to terms with his inner self. This accomplishment is achieved when a wounding of the ego and the suffering which follow occur.

In the latest issue of the magazine <u>Working Mother</u>, an article entitled *"The New Achievers"* by Susan Seliger reported the results of a survey conducted in June 1997. The question asked was, "How ambitious are you?" 27% answered highly ambitious, 65% said they were ambitious, and 8% said they were not ambitious. The report goes on to say that a generation ago, women were reluctant to admit their ambitions, for fear they would be called unwomanly.

Nowadays, there is a change happening. This shift, which is called "Entropy" in psychological terms, will continue until completed. It is a natural evolutionary cycle. So it is best that we men recognize this, accept it, and assist it until balance has been achieved.

The magazine Working Mother has only recently been put on the market. It addresses concerns of working mothers today. Now, my mother was a working mother almost 50 years ago, long before there were organizations and magazines to help women plan their lives. 50 years ago, my brothers and I learned to cook, wash clothes, iron shirts, and clean the house. We did the inside work as well as the outside work -- haul hay, feed livestock, etc. My father would take care of us boys when mother went to summer school. The secret to success in our life was the sharing of duties. There were no girl duties or boy duties in our house. You just did what you were good at. In the old days, a person would go on a vision quest to find out what he was good at or what his purpose in life might be. Today, we use astrology. Astrology is a picture of the heavens the moment you are born. From this picture or Star Map, a skilled astrologer can determine a person's inclinations for his life. As we move into the next century, many educators are at a loss about how to teach the youth. I feel that astrology is a valuable tool that could be used in education. In the old days, astrology was considered a joke and teaching was by reward and punishment.

Today, entropy is occurring and things are changing. Innovative teaching techniques are being introduced. My mother was ahead of her time when she used whole brain (hands on) teaching methodology. My mother set standards not only for herself, but for her sex, which later became goals for other women. My mother, until this book came out, has never boasted of her achievements; she just lived her life, and without knowing, has helped others through her example. That is a truly remarkable trait.

Ho Hecatu Yelo
"That's the way it is."

Mitakuye Oyasin
"We are all related."

EPILOGUE

Moira Timms states in her book *Beyond Prophecies and Predictions* that a Mars, Uranus/Neptune conjunction in Aquarius, December 1999, will provide, for mankind, energy for an increase in spiritual based unity. As this dissolving of superficial differences and a tolerant attitude for all races occurs, the Divine Mother will rise in her fullness. The presiding male force will then move into a more harmonic relationship with the feminine. Timms goes on to say that starting in December 1994 Pluto/Jupiter in Scorpio will provide energy for educational institutions to begin important changes. Jupiter, the sign of higher mind/philosophies, will create a general acceptance of new knowledge and truth.

Since my first field of study was in education and my secondary field in esoteric sciences, I can see how this book is the fulfillment of the astrological prophecies stated above.

From my book, *Mitakuye Oyasin*, I remembered the following:

> "The New age is identified as the millennium of which the Bible speaks, according to Ruth Montgomery. "In the New Age," she said, "all mankind will be brothers, without regard to race, sex, or creed." She further delineated that in the next age, the learning process will be speeded up. Books will be read almost at a glance, and the material contained within will be absorbed through mental osmosis. Our school systems will be changed dramatically. A person will be able to get the information he needs by tapping directly into the minds of others rather than by attending school for twelve years."

When I first read Montgomery's prophecies, I could not fathom how such changes were possible. Ten years have passed since I first read her prophecies and I am now beginning to understand the possibilities for the future.

Gordon Michael-Scallion states in the *Earth Changes Report* that what is happening now (1998) is a Great Awakening. This is made possible by an expansion of the centers of the brain, for an increased interaction between the Dream state, Archetypal world of the masses, and the memory of everything that has been experienced. One might say that the intelligence of mankind is rising.

Scallion goes on to say that,

"The present educational systems throughout the globe will collapse before 2001, partially as a result of the greater Earth changes, but also because those systems will no longer support the needs of the shifting mass consciousness. The new global education system will begin with small community groups."

At the beginning of 1998, Timms also writes, there will be a major planetary conjunction of Sun, Moon, Mercury, Jupiter, Neptune, and Uranus, all in Aquarius. This conjunction will release a pro-evolutionary (New Age) energy into the world's collective consciousness. This energy will provide strong influences that will assist our <u>individuation</u>.

I feel this book is very "timely" in an effort to provide awareness for global changes. It gives one a clear picture of what can be achieved if one has a tolerant attitude and patience -- inclinations my mother has had all her life.

BIBLIOGRAPHY

Anderson, Gary Clayton. Little Crow Spokesman for the Sioux. St. Paul, Minnesota Historical Society Press, 1986.

Ballentine, Betty and Ian Ballentine, eds. The Native Americans: An Illustrated History. Turner Publishing, 1993.

Billard, Jules B., ed. The World of the American Indian. The National Geographic Society Press, 1993.

Bonvillain, Nancy. The Santee Sioux. Philadelphia, Chelsea House Publishers, 1997.

Campbell, Joseph. The Portable Jung. New York, Penguin Group Publishing, 1976.

Deloria, Ella Cara. Speaking of Indians. New York, Friendship Press, 1988.

Eastman, Charles. The Soul of the Indian. San Rafael, New World Library Press, 1993.

Friedan, Betty. The Feminine Mystique. New York, Dell Publishing, 1983.

Green, Rayna. Women in American Indian Society. New York, Chelsea House Publishers, 1992.

Hall, Calvin S. and Nordby, Vernon J. A Primer of Jungian Psychology. New York, New American Library Press, 1973.

Meyer, Roy W. History of the Santee Sioux, United States Indian Policy on Trial. Lincoln, University of Nebraska Press, 1967.

Ross, Dr. A.C. Ehanamani. Wicòni Wastè, 1992.

Ross, Dr. A.C. Mitakuye Oyasin "We are all related". Wicòni Wastè, 1989.

Scallion, Gordon Michael. Notes from the Cosmos. Chesterfield, Matrix Institute Press, 1997.

Sneve, Virginia Driving Hawk. Completing the Circle, Lincoln, University of Nebraska Press, 1995.

"The Great Awakening." Earth Changes Report, Dec 1997.

Timms, Moira. Beyond Prophecies and Predictions. Ballantine Books, New York, 1994.

PHOTOGRAPHIC CREDITS

The photographs and images appear through the courtesy of the people and in the situations listed below.

Family Genealogy Chart, p. 146-150. Jim Bill Ross.

Little Crow, p. 48. (A.Z. Shindler) National Anthropological Archives, Smithsonian Institute.

Minnesota Reservation Map, p. 26. Allen Ross.

Wowinape, p. 41. (J.E. Whitney) Minnesota Historical Society.

All other photographs - Agnes Ross' personal collection.

MITAKUYE OYASIN

"We are all related"

The history and culture of America before Columbus, based on American Indian oral history. Twenty-six years of research have gone into this book. It is the doctorate dissertation of Lakota Sioux author, Ehanamani "walks among."

The book **MITAKUYE OYASIN** by Ehanamani A. C. Ross compares the legends and cultures of the American Indian with the world's major philosophies and religions.

Topics include:

- Esoteric teachings of the American Indian
- Brain hemisphercy and cultural attitudes
- Spiritual healing
- Black Elk's prophecy
- Strategies for global harmony
- American Indian philosophy
- Origins of the American Indian

ISBN 0-9621977-0X $14.95

MITAKUYE OYASIN
"We are all related"
America before columbus,
based on the oral history of 34 tribes.

REVISED EDITION
Ehanamani
(Dr. A.C. Ross)

Winner of the 1992 "top 50" Recognition Award at the Frankfurt International Bookfair, **MITAKUYE OYASIN** is being used in over 50 universities and 300 high schools in the areas of: psychology, comparative religions, native American studies, philosophy, counseling and guidance.

In its twelfth printing, the book is a best seller in Europe with translations in French, Russian, German, Japanese and Italian.

A teacher's guide is also available.

EHANAMANI
"WALKS AMONG"

THE STORY OF A SUNDANCE CHIEF

FOLLOW THE EHANAMANI FAMILY FROM 1863 WHEN IT WAS FORCED ONTO THE RESERVATION AND LEARN ABOUT RESERVATION LIFE FROM 1940 TO THE PRESENT.

YOU'LL LEARN:

1. THE REAL REASON THE THE SLOGAN "INDIAN GIVER".

2. ABOUT THE CHIEF BIG FOOT RIDE PROPHECY.

3. ABOUT THE SERPENT VISION.

4. WHAT THE TERM WALK - IN MEANS.

5. HOW AMERICAN INDIAN POVERTY IS PERPETUATED.

6. HOW ENCOUNTERS OF THE FOURTH KIND ARE GUIDING US INTO THE FUTURE.

ISBN 0-9621977-2-6 $12.00

Ehanamani
"Walks Among"

The story of a Sun Dance Chief

CRAZY HORSE

and

The Real Reason for the Battle of the Little Big Horn

A new book by Dr. A. Ross Ehanamani

Book Contains Several Firsts

- It is the only book about Crazy Horse and The Battle of the Little Big Horn, written by a Sioux author.
- Identifies Crazy Horse's actual birthplace
- Battle of Little Big Horn, based on oral history of the warriors who fought against Custer
- Battle maps drawn according to information given by the warriors who were at the battle
- Identifies exact location where Custer was shot
- Identifies the "last stand" area of the soldiers
- This book is unique in that Native American ceremonialism was utilized to contact the spirit realm for information to supplement the historical research.

ISBN 0-9621977 - 8 - 5

$12.00

AMERICAN INDIAN PROPHECIES I

(Ojibwa, Hopi, Paiute, Sioux, Maya, Navajo, and Aztec)

Compared with predictions by:

NOSTRADAMUS
EDGAR CAYCE
RUTH MONTGOMERY
GORDON-MICHAEL SCALLION

Produced by Wicóni Wasté
Narrated by Dr. A.C. Ross
Author of <u>Mitakuye Oyasin</u>
"We are all related"

DISCOVER:

Δ How to prepare for the coming earth changes
Δ How the Black Hills can be returned
Δ When spiritual unity will occur
Δ What to invest money in for the future
Δ What is causing the increase in earthquakes, volcanic eruptions, and unknown diseases

HOME VIDEO

VHS - $19.95 + $3.95(S&H) = $23.90
PAL (European) - $29.95 + $8.95(S&H) = $38.90
(We accept Visa/MC)

MAIL ORDER

SEND TO: **Wicóni Wasté " Beautiful Life"**
P.O. Box 480005
Denver, CO 80248
303-238-3420

AMERICAN INDIAN PROPHECIES I
Wicóni Wasté – copyright 1996

AMERICAN INDIAN PROPHECIES I

Sun Dance Vision

Produced by:
Wicóni Wasté
Running Time 1 hr.

AMERICAN INDIAN PROPHECIES II

An Interview With "Ehanamani"

a.k.a.

Dr. A.C. Ross

Due to popular demand, Dr. Ross discusses the prophecies presented in the video, American Indian Prophecies I

Interviewer: John Belindo

Issues to be Discussed:

△ Return of the White Buffalo
△ The Mayan calendar's connection to the "Quickening."
△ Biblical prophecy comparisons
△ When will spiritual unity occur
△ Will Tribal Governments survive
△ Black Elk's Vision of the Flowering Tree
△ Who is guiding us into the next century

HOME VIDEO

<u>MAIL ORDER</u>

VHS - $19.95 + $3.95 (S&H) = $23.90
PAL (European) - $29.95 + $8.95 (S&H) = $38.90
(We accept **Visa/MC**)

SEND TO: Wicóni Wasté "Beautiful Life"
P.O. Box 480005
Denver, CO 80248
303-238-3420

AMERICAN INDIAN PROPHECIES II
Wicóni Wasté – copyright 1996

ISBN 0-9621977-1-2

9 780962 197741   51995>

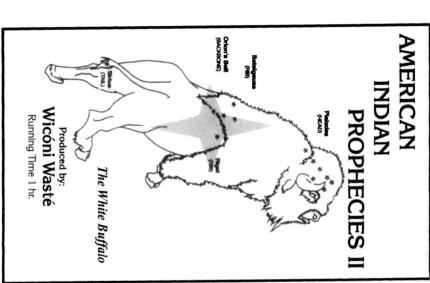

AMERICAN INDIAN PROPHECIES II

Pleiades
(HEAD)

Orion's Belt
(BACKBONE)

Betelgeuse
(TAIL)

Sirius
(TAIL)

Rigel

The White Buffalo

Produced by:
Wicóni Wasté
Running Time 1 hr.

AMERICAN INDIAN PROPHECIES III

An Interview With "Ehanamani"

a.k.a.

Dr. A.C. Ross

Due to popular demand, Dr. Ross discusses
additional prophecies

Interviewer: Jeff D. Alley

Issues to be Discussed:

Δ Black Elk's Sacred Hoop of Nations Vision
Δ Will the Sweat Lodge Ceremony Survive?
Δ Dawson No Horse Vision of the Future
Δ Prophecy of the androgynous beings
Δ What is meant by "medium of exchange"
Δ A dream about the American Indian Prophecy videos
Δ Wounded Knee memorial ride prophecy

MAIL ORDER

HOME VIDEO

VHS - $19.95 + $3.95 (S&H) = $23.90
PAL (European) - $29.95 + $8.95 (S&H) = $38.90
(We accept Visa/MC)

SEND TO: **Wicóni Wasté "Beautiful Life"**
          P.O. Box 480005
          Denver, CO 80248
          303-238-3420

AMERICAN INDIAN PROPHECIES III

Wounded Knee Memorial Ride Prophecy

Produced by:
Wicóni Wasté
Running Time 55 min.

HALE - BOPP
COMET OR STAR?

A Presentation by Ehanamani

a.k.a.

Dr. A.C. Ross

△ A Comparison of information concerning the HALE – BOPP comet.

Topics Presented:

△ Learn the correlation between the Blue Star and the comet Hale – Bopp.

△ What do the Hopi / Lakota have in common with the Blue Star.

△ Discover the connection between the Bible and Hale – Bopp

△ Is Hale – Bopp a harbinger for destruction or peace?

△ Why has NASA discontinued publishing information concerning Hale – Bopp?

△ Is there a correlation between Hale – Bopp and the 12th planet?

△ Learn how Hale – Bopp is ushering in the second coming.

<u>MAIL ORDER</u>

HOME VIDEO

VHS - $19.95 + $3.95(S&H) = $23.90

PAL (European) - $29.95 + $8.95(S&H) = $38.90

(We accept Visa/MC)

SEND TO: **Wicóni Wasté " Beautiful Life "**
P.O. Box 480005
Denver, CO 80248
303-238-3420

HALE - BOPP: COMET OR STAR?
Wicóni Wasté – copyright 1997

ISBN 0-962197-6-9
9 780962 197765
5 19995 >

HALE - BOPP

COMET OR STAR?

Produced by:
Wicóni Wasté
Running Time 1 hour

BOOKS

	ORDER FORM		
	Name _____		
	Address _____		
	City _____ State _____ Zip _____		

Qty	Title	Price/Video	Total
	EHANAMANI	$12.00 EA	
	MITAKUYE OYASIN	$14.95 EA	
	KEEPER OF THE FEMALE MEDICINE BUNDLE	$14.95 EA	
	CRAZY HORSE	$12.00 EA	
	THE HERO	$19.95 EA	
		SUBTOTAL	
		Postage (see below)	
	Handling ($1.50 per order)		
		TOTAL	

Postage

1-4 copies	$5.15
5-8 copies	additional $5.15

For other international orders, add $8.00 per book.

Make checks, money orders and
purchase orders payable to:

Allen Ross
PO BOX 480005
DENVER, CO 80248

DVD
MAIL ORDER FORM

American Indian Prophecy Videos I, II, III and IV

ORDER FORM			
Name _____			
Address _____			
City _____ State _____ Zip _____			

Qty.	Title	Price / DVD	Total
	DVD	$19.95 EA	
	SET (4 DVD's)	$59.95 EA	
	American Indian Star Connections DVD	$24.99 EA	
POSTAGE (BOOK RATE)			
	DVD	$ 5.15 EA	
	1 SET (4 DVD's)	$ 5.15	
	Handling ($1.50 per order)		$ 1.50
TOTAL			

Air Mail: For orders from outside the USA, add $5.00 per DVD. For orders from outside North America, add $8.00 per DVD.

Make checks, money orders and purchase orders payable to:

Allen Ross
PO Box 480005
Denver, CO 80248

ABOUT THE AUTHOR

Ehanamani (Walks Among) aka A.C. Ross has worked for 27 years in the field of education as a teacher, principal, superintendent, college professor and college department chairman.
He left formal education to promote his book entitled *MITA-KUYE OYASIN - We Are All Related.* It won the top book award in Europe's largest book fair in 1992. It is now a best seller in its 33rd printing with over 100,000 copies sold.

A.C.Ross' second book *EHANAMANI "Walks among"* is in the 10th printing. His third book *KEEPER OF THE FEMALE MEDICINE BUNDLE* is in the 10th printing, and *CRAZY HORSE* is in his 4th book.

A.C. Ross has lectured on cultural understanding in 44 states in the U.S., 7 Canadian provinces, 8 European countries and most recently, Japan.